W

I was shocked to hear that Pastor Mike was this hip, like seriously. This book is the reason why young millennials like myself can understand the power and word of God. God isn't meant to be unreachable or non-relatable. If we all have God in us that means God been hip and that's where we get it from. I appreciate the stance on addressing the "which side are you on?" stigma when it comes to being a Christian or being a hip-hop lover. Why has there been debates on being both? Why can't you? Pastor Mike touches a very controversial subject as it relates to religion and music and brings it all together to makes it make sense. This is truly The Holy Bible (Hip-Hop Version) with a few letters from apostle "P Mike" and low key has the power to bring a lot of us younger people towards God without feeling ashamed of being who we are and loving what we love... at the same d*** time "Future voice."

— EVAN "X" JOHNSON, founder of Timeless Recording Studios and award-winning music producer

Concurrently rich in God and Hip-Hop, Dr. Michael Scruggs' knack for entwining his love for Jesus and love for the culture masterfully provides the blueprint detailing how the Church and Hip-Hop immensely intersect. Intentionality at its finest, you'll find yourself breath taken by laughter one minute and subsequently awestruck by mic drop worthy inspiration. His pen game rivals the best of emcees. Monographically a must read.

— REGIS "K-DRAMA" JONES,
Billboard charting recording artist

"All rappers want to be preachers and all preachers want to be rappers." Yo, Dr. Mike Scruggs just broke down the theology of hip hop for those of us who know it best--especially those of us who wrestle with everything it does for us and to us. If you grew up learning how to cope using cassette tapes or CD's you kept in shoeboxes, know all the bars to Wu Tang, Rakim, or NWA, and you've gone to extremes to deal with the distance between hip hop and your faith, this is your book. If you know there's more to hip hop culture than beats and rhymes, this is your book. Dr. Scruggs reflects on the complexity of hip hop's history, its diverse religious and economic connections, and pauses to consider the application of its lessons from a place of realism and appreciation. From the lyrics to the shout outs, Dr. Scruggs uses his wit, his humor, and his love for people in the struggle to teach us something important about hip hop and through hip hop in a way that helps reclaim the part of the "culture" that we need most.

— PASTOR MIKE JR., founder and senior pastor
of Rock City Church and national recording artist

THE **RAP**ture

THE **RAP**ture

THE THIN LINE BETWEEN GOD AND HIP-HOP

DR. MICHAEL SCRUGGS

LINER NOTES

Yeah, this book is dedicated to all the teachers that told me I'd never amount to nothin'.

To all the people that lived above the buildings that I was hustlin' in front of. Called the police on me when I was just tryin' to make some money to feed my daughter.

And all the authors in the struggle. You know what I'm sayin'? It's all good, baby baby!

It was all a dream…

TRACKLISTING

40 side north

41st side south

40 side north

C.L. FRANKLIN AND CL SMOOTH

I got licensed to preach in 1979, the same year that hip-hop got its sea legs as it cruised onto the American music charts after first launching its bid for relevance in the spirited vessel of Black pop culture in the Bronx in 1973. On November 21, 1979, in Detroit, Michigan, a month after my 21st birthday, I preached my first sermon, "The Body Christian: The Vital Connection," crafting a theology of the church as I belatedly began, two months earlier, my freshman year at Knoxville College.

I had become a teen father in 1978 in the Motor City, delaying by four years my full entrée into higher education. In the meantime, I worked as an arc welder in a wheel brake and drum factory, clerked in a wood forms shop at Chrysler, and after that, picked up odd jobs shoveling snow, painting houses, cutting grass and laboring as an emergency substitute janitor in the Detroit Public Schools. In between I stood in long lines at WIC (Women, Infants and Children) to collect food as a proxy for my wife. On September 16, 1979, the Sugarhill Gang released "Rapper's Delight," the first hip-hop single to climb into the top 40 and introduce a wider audience to the fledgling art form.

My fatherhood, ministry, and higher education began at the same time that hip-hop emerged. Thus, I have always seen one through the lens of the other. I have viewed fatherhood through parenting, ministry, and scholarship; I saw ministry through fatherhood, intellectual labor, and rap music; I viewed scholarship through hip-hop, religious thought, and Black masculinity; and I looked at hip-hop through Black fatherhood, Black sacred speech, and Black intellectual work. Since each provided a check and balance on the other, I wasn't burdened with the usual tensions between sacred and secular forces that plague many believers.

The absence of such brutal discord may be explained by the greater tension that already existed between faith and reason, between the gospel preaching I heard in Black churches and the critical perspective on religious truth encouraged in the university. That dispute long predated the quarrels between rap and religion.

The conflict between listening to C.L. Franklin and CL Smooth, for instance, was not so much understood as an intellectual disagreement as much as a moral one. This moral dissension between the two might have been seen as the battle between the edifying ethical views of a preacher who was pastor of New Bethel Baptist Church in Detroit, and the gritty gutter level views of an emcee reared in New Rochelle, New York. The church and the streets are certainly at odds, but there are also moments of unanticipated convergence, as when the prophet writes in Isaiah 50:4 that, "He awakens Me morning by morning," and as Scarface raps, in "What Can I Do?" that, "I thank the Lord, for every morning he allows me to rise."[1]

There are also moments of revealing contrast. For example, when it comes to death, and mourning the memory of the departed, C.L. Franklin warned against the belief that we are irreplaceable, preaching, in his sermon, "The King Lord of Hosts," that "God has some successors to us" and that we shouldn't "think that the world is going to stop because we happen to stop, or pass on."[2] CL Smooth, on the other hand, mourned his fallen comrade by suggesting the immortal impression made by his life, and the witness of such a life, declaring that "I reminisce so you never forget this/The days way back, so many bear witness."[3]

To be sure, there are many hostilities between hip-hop and religious belief, most visibly, those that flow from the failure of rap artists to hold women in high regard. I was in the awkward position of defending the freedom of speech of hip-hoppers while sitting on a Congressional panel and gently

---

[1] Scarface, Kelly Price and T-Mix, *"What Can I Do"*, released August 6, 2002, track 7 on *The Fix*, The Island Def Jam Music Group, https://genius.com/Scarface-what-can-i-do-lyrics.

[2] C.L. Franklin, The King Lord of Hosts/King of The Jews, 2008, Gospel AIR Records & Tapes AIR7047, compact disc.

[3] Pete Rock and C.L. Smooth, *"They Reminisce Over You (T.R.O.Y.)"*, released April 1994, track 10 on *Mecca and The Soul Brother*, Elektra Entertainment Group & Elektra Records, https://genius.com/Pete-rock-and-cl-smooth-they-reminisce-over-you-troy-lyrics.

sparring with the great songstress Dionne Warwick and the late politician and social activist C. Delores Tucker. I understood their dispute with artists who aimed venom and malevolence at the vulnerable bodies of Black women.

This antagonism was clear to me when I was dispatched by Vibe magazine in 1993 to do a story on the late Reverend Calvin Butts, then pastor of Harlem's historic Abyssinian Baptist Church, who threatened to steamroll the compact discs of artists like Snoop Dogg. As a Baptist preacher, I had profound empathy with Butts's pastoral care of women, even as I challenged the deeply rooted misogyny that mocked the church sanctuary. I never published my article, and Butts and I struck up a friendship that lasted until his death 30 years later in 2023.

The Black church may loudly denounce hip-hop's horrid sexism, but it has rarely come to grips with its own misogyny and patriarchy. The bulk of the membership in most Black churches is composed of women, and yet it is still all too rare that they assume leadership at the top of the holy hierarchy. No, women are surely not called out of their names at church, but they are denied placing their hands on the levers of power to determine what policies and practices prevail. Despite their much smaller numbers, men still rule the day. There is a far more extensive tradition of male supremacy operating in church than in hip hop, and what makes it worse is that it all seems to be sanctioned by The Spirit – at least in the preaching and theology of too many pastors.

The beautiful thing about The RAPture is that Pastor Scruggs has a holistic theology of engagement with the truths that are revealed in hip-hop, drawing his principles from scripture while never being harnessed to a deadened literalism. Yes, he has a definite point of view, but there is neither self-righteousness at play, nor a vain dismissal of the competing insights of hip-hop culture because they traffic in obscenities and vulgarities. Yet Pastor Scruggs understands that as bad as those offenses may be, they pale in comparison to the obscene social forces and vulgar politics that complicate Black lives.

The book wonderfully forces us to think for ourselves. It challenges us to rip the veil from our eyes that prevents us from acknowledging the sins that circulate in our congregations. And it invites us to grapple with the shortcomings that too often shape the rituals and routines of our faith. Hip-hop offers a great deal of insight about the traumas and terrors that Black folk have faced throughout our pilgrimage on American soil. Yes, hip-hop culture at times glorifies the violent self-destruction that plagues the Black world. And yet, it offers trenchant observations about the ugly truths we can scarcely afford to ignore.

We church folk are appalled when gay rapper Lil Nas X makes a song, and accompanying video, entitled "MONTERO (Call Me By Your Name), that pictures him joyously descending into hell to seduce the Devil. Yet we take no responsibility for telling queer folk that they are going straight to hell. 2Pac had decades earlier decried the hypocrisy of the church sending folk to hell for their sins, asking, "Have you ever seen a crackhead?

That's eternal fire,"[4] linking the predicament of addiction to the social malaise of race and class.

Pastor Scruggs pulls no punches and wrestles mightily with the demons of denial, the devils of distraction, and the serpents of suffering that beleaguer Black culture inside the church and within the hip-hop cypher. He measures our faith in God, and how hip-hop can menace us or minister to our needs, all while refusing to throw out the rhetorical baby with the bathwater of polluted spirits. After all, preachers and griots, and emcees and evangelists, face the same set of temptations as they go about their duties. Will money corrupt them? Will success blind them? Will prosperity make them fatally self-centered? Will acceptance by the powers that be blunt their prophetic edges?

The church and hip-hop have even more in common. Both leverage the moral and political genius of Black life to the advantage of the most vulnerable members of our communities. If we cannot make certain that those who have been shut out, left out, and put out of our loving communion are invited back in, then neither our sacred spaces nor our artistic spheres can claim to be healing places for the culture. If we do not love our people by challenging the injustices of our society, then, despite our eloquent speech, we are, as Paul says in 1 Corinthians, uttering words that are but "sounding brass, or a tinkling cymbal."

---

[4] 2Pac, Prince Ital Joe and Hurt-M-Badd, *"Blasphemy"*, released 1996, track 8 on *The Don Killumanati: The 3 Day Theory,* Death Row Records & Interscope Records, https://genius.com/2pac-blasphemy-lyrics.

In short, words that are empty and confusing. Then we will be forced to ask, with JAY-Z, "Where's the love?"[5]

Pastor Scruggs brilliantly probes the interface between church and rap, between God and hip-hop, and between the world where C.L. Franklin can preach and CL Smooth can spit knowledge, and where both men are joined in common struggle against the forces that harm and oppress us. That, surely, is worth a hearty "Amen."

Michael Eric Dyson,
New York Times bestselling author
and Vanderbilt University Professor

[5] Jay-Z, et al., *"Heart of the City (Ain't No Love)"*, released September 11, 2001, track 8 on *The Blueprint,* Roc-A-Fella Records, https://genius.com/Jay-z-heart-of-the-city-aint-no-love-lyrics.

PRELUDE

I met this girl when I was 10 years old
And what I loved most she had so much soul
She was old school when I was just a shorty
Never knew throughout my life
she would be there for me
On the regular, not a church girl, she was secular

Common, *I Used to Love H.E.R.*[1]

I love hip-hop. I also hate her. That is, if you can anthropomorphically assign a genre of music a gender. You see, we grew up together. We were there for each other during the good and the bad. The highs and the lows. Along the way, I became fully aware of "Dave the Dope Fiend's" lack of knowledge of water and soap, how to sport New Balance sneakers to avoid a narrow path, that "there is no future in your frontin'" and I quickly discovered the difference between bad meaning *bad* and bad meaning *good*. However, I also learned that there are ten commandments to crack dealing, that it's hard

---

[1] Common and No I.D., "*I Used to Love H.E.R.*", released September 1994, track 2 on *Resurrection*, Relativity Records, https://genius.com/Common-i-used-to-love-her-lyrics.

out here for a pimp, and that gin should always be accompanied with some type of juice.

During my journey with hip-hop, I have been able to travel from Queens to Compton and from Orange Mound to Carol City, all from the comfort of my bedroom. She birthed my dichotomous personality. I am a poor, righteous teacher as well as a nigga with an attitude. To quote rapper, Derek Minor, "I'm somewhere between Martin Luther King and '99 Master P."[2] And did I mention, I also love Jesus?

That's right, despite being, or though I felt, forced to go to church as a child, I actually fell in love with Jesus as a late teen. I was leading youth groups. I held titles and offices in different Christian organizations. And I now currently pastor a wonderful church in Cincinnati, Ohio. But unlike others who gave their heart over to the Lord, I never changed my listening preferences. I simply segregated them.

The first gospel cassette tape I owned was Kirk Franklin's God's Property project. I would listen to Nas, OutKast or Eightball and MJG all week long, up to the point of pulling within a block of the church parking lot on Sunday morning, and then switch over to *Stomp*. I just figured there was "a time for everything." Even now, while at the gym, I'm more apt to have Pusha T in my playlist than Mahalia Jackson. Jeezy

---

[2] Derek Minor, *"Fresh Prince"*, released June 30, 2017, Derek Minor's House, https://genius.com/Derek-minor-fresh-prince-lyrics.

helps me a little more on the treadmill than Fred Hammond. Sorry, Fred!

Hip-hop music, when done right, has the amazing ability to speak prophetically to a generation of young people that desperately lack insight on a system designed to keep them enslaved. But it simultaneously perpetuates stereotypes of African-Americans that are then emulated in every facet of media.

For the first time since Nielsen started measuring music consumption in the United States, rock is no longer the top genre in terms of overall consumption. Hip-hop has taken the crown.[3]

Growing up in the 1980's afforded me the unique opportunity to be a part of the first generation of pastors that were reared and raised on hip-hop. My parent's generation was Motown. Their parents' generation was blues driven.

I remember growing up watching my father go to the basement and put on records, piping music throughout the house. Because my father and mother listened to certain music, by default, I grew to like what they liked. I remember the sounds of Rick James, Aretha Franklin, the Gap Band, and a sprinkling of the Lionel Richie led Commodores singing, *Jesus is Love*, for that touch of church every now and then. I remember how it felt

---

[3] Hugh McIntyre, "Report: Hip-Hop/R&B Is the Dominant Genre in the U.S. for the First Time," Forbes (Forbes Magazine, July 17, 2017), https://www.forbes.com/sites/hughmcintyre/2017/07/17/hip-hoprb-has-now-become-the-dominant-genre-in-the-u-s-for-the-first-time/.

to dance to those sounds and feel good all over without a care in the world. It's not like any of our problems went away. Our problems were still there, but for six minutes and eleven seconds *Brick House* drowned them out.

While I have vivid recollections of my father playing James Brown and the Isley Brothers, as I got older, my palate for music evolved. My first cassette tapes, dating back to elementary school, consisted of the Beastie Boys, Eazy-E and Too $hort. When my mother would go in a store and leave me in the car, I would slide in *Life is...Too $hort* until she returned. If I was forced to go in the store, I would hang by the magazine aisle reading *Right On!*, and later got subscriptions to *The Source*, *Vibe*, and *XXL*.

Fast forward, to a couple years ago, my family and I moved to a new house, and in the process of packing, I parted ways with stacks of magazines that I had accumulated over the years, many of which I had a relationship with longer than I did with my wife. Needless to say, I almost chose the magazines!

In my mind, 2 Chainz and I are friends. Although we have never met, I felt some type of way that I did not officiate his wedding. In this alternate reality, I lay out my clothes the night before going to the Roc Nation brunch and Killer Mike and I banter about having the same name. I wonder why Chance doesn't DM me regarding bible study topics. Or why I wasn't asked to share some words of comfort at Phife's or DMX's funerals.

My life is forever linked to hip-hop. It is a part of my DNA. When you converse with me, hip-hop references come out of me naturally based on years of being inculcated in the culture. I'm old enough to know Run D.M.C., but still young enough to quote Meek Mill.

Was all of that supposed to change once I gave my life to Christ? Am I less of a Christian because I can quote just as many Bible verses as I can Notorious B.I.G. verses? Many would consider me a theologian, but I can more easily name all ten members of the Wu-Tang Clan quicker than I can Jesus' twelve disciples (I start with the intro to *Method Man* and then add Cappadonna and Masta Killa). Even if I steamrolled all of my CDs, according to Calvin Butt's wishes[4], how does one steamroll some of their fondest memories? I kept my cassette tapes in shoeboxes. Next to a tape of my first sermon is the original single release of Notorious B.I.G.'s *One More Chance*.

I do this for my culture.

This book is for those that grew up in two different households, hip-hop and church, but find themselves with divided loyalties when it comes to choosing whom to live with, because, of course, there are different rules for each house.

---

[4] Clifford J. Levy, "Harlem Protest of Rap Lyrics Draws Debate and Steamroller," The New York Times, June 6, 1993, https://www.nytimes.com/1993/06/06/nyregion/harlem-protest-of-rap-lyrics-draws-debate-and-steamroller.html.

This book is also for products of "single-parent homes." You saw nothing wrong with your upbringing, because you know Rakim and Soulja Boy (shout out to Big Draco!) did their best in raising you with what they had. It is not until later in life that you realize there were some things missing you wished you had. When drugs, violence, hypermasculinity and misogyny have been normalized, it is hard to come out of this home unscathed.

This book is for every "b-girl" that tried to find their identity in hip-hop while hip-hop was trying to find its identity in itself. So, you were either "on that tip about stoppin' the violence" or you were a "gangsta rollin' with gangsta b******."

This book is for those that believe "segregation now, segregation tomorrow, segregation forever." That hip-hop is evil and there is no way to bridge it AND faith.

As we navigate hip-hop's origins, I incorporate how God's people had a hand in its creation, evolution and stigmatization. There is no hip-hop without the involvement of Muslims and Jews. Christians are a guest in this house. And because of this boarder status, it still has awkward encounters with the rest of the family.

There is something spiritual about music that transcends 808s, breakbeats, chords, loops, and hi-hats. Something that precedes time itself. As we navigate this book together, I want to show how if you believe God is the progenitor of everything, and that "the earth is the Lord's, and everything in it"[5], then music has to fall into that category, in particular hip-hop. And if so, there is a line that both segregates and joins God and hip-hop together that is worth exploring. So, "let us begin, what, where, why or when…"

---

[5] Psalm 24:1 (KJV)

THE GENESIS

You love to hear the story again and again
Of how it all got started way back when

MC Shan, *The Bridge*[1]

When you look at the timeline of music, the music of a particular era tends to reflect the attitudes of the people of that time, and vice-versa. Looking specifically at African-Americans, songs like *Say It Loud – I'm Black and I'm Proud, Soul Power,* and *For God's Sake (Give More Power To The People)*, spoke of being confident in your stride and appearance, and not relinquishing your God-given authority to be free mentally, physically or spiritually.

The civil rights movement, initiated to draw attention to the injustices imposed on African-Americans in the South, was the most striking protest movement of the 1960s, if not of all time. It attracted the social segments that were concerned about alienation, war, ecology and religious evangelism and had the "call to arms" effect of bringing the generations together. The

---

[1] MC Shan and Marley Marl, *"The Bridge"*, released August 1987, track 3 on *Down By Law,* Cold Chillin'/Warner Bros. Records, https://genius.com/Mc-shan-the-bridge-lyrics.

potency of the rallies was stimulated by a cultural element. Here you had a political movement in which the primary participants, disenfranchised Black people of all ages, were unified by a common religious and musical experience: a tradition of earnest congregational singing.

The most familiar song of the movement, still sung at rallies and gatherings to this day, and one of the most widely known songs of our time is, *We Shall Overcome*. It originates from a turn of the century hymn. The tempo is slow, the tune is easy to sing and it is full of repetition. The leader or initiator of the song has the power and prerogative to input topical lines to a sympathetic audience and make a powerful impact.

Every generation had a spokesperson that would shed light on the struggles of their people via music. This dates all the way back to the psalms of David, Solomon and Asaph. Bob Marley and Gill Scott Herron spoke for their time. James Brown spoke for his. Even with the emergence of hip-hop, its creation was based on bringing the current situations of the time to light and speaking truth to power. Hip-hop got its start less than a decade after a defining and cataclysmic event: The death of Martin Luther King, Jr. King's death rocked our culture like few deaths ever have.[2]

Depending on who you ask, hip-hop's point of origin dates back to August 11, 1973 in the Bronx borough of New

---

[2] Monica R. Miller, Bernard 'Bun B' Freeman, and Anthony B. Pinn, *Religion in Hip Hop* (New York, NY: Bloomsbury Academic, 2015).

York City. It was there that DJ Kool Herc was on the turntables during a party at 1520 Sedgwick Avenue. The lesser known (to the outside world) master of ceremonies, Coke La Rock, was on the mic and that poignant night led to a cultural movement that has amended the status quo and how we do life — from cereal to politics.

In the United States, the second Tuesday in November is considered election day. Public officials are elected on that day. However, they are not installed or inaugurated until January. One has to think of hip-hop like this, it had been anticipated, but its official arrival took place at a birthday party hosted by Herc.

Nelson George notes, "rap or something like it should have been predicted. Each decade since World War II has seen the emergence of some new approach to black dance music and more, I suspect. The 1940s brought forth rhythm & blues, the 1950s rock & roll, the 1960s soul, the 1970s funk and disco. Something was due in the 1980s."[3]

Henry Louis Gates defines hip-hop as "a set of formal qualities, an iconoclastic spirit, and a virtuosic sense of wordplay. It extends the long-standing practice in the African-American oral tradition of language games." [4] It brought

---

[3] Anthony B. Pinn, *Noise and Spirit: The Religious and Spiritual Sensibilities of Rap Music* (New York, NY: New York University Press, 2003).

[4] Adam Bradley and Andrew Lee Dubois, eds., *The Anthology of Rap* (New Haven, CT: YALE University Press, 2011), p. 23.

together without apology jazz, disco, rhythm & blues, and so on; and in the process, through high-tech conjuration, presented musical ancestors within a new context.[5]

But before there was a Cardi B or an Offset, there was Pigmeat Markham, Rudy Ray Moore, Gil Scott-Heron and James Brown. Lest we forget Grandmaster Flowers, Nu Sounds, and King Charles. And even they drew their roots from Caribbean and West Indian sound clashes and West African musicians telling stories rhythmically, with the accompaniment of a drum.

Hip-hop has become a phenomenon throughout the world over. What was assumed to be a fad has grown from a house party to a multi-billion-dollar global industry, that serves as an umbrella for not just music, but fashion, television, movies, and even video games, creating international superstars and hip-hop moguls along the way. Hip-hop has probably generated more millionaires than any college has, to the point where hip-hop is now taught in college! Rappers are the closest thing the ghetto has to superheroes.

Most people under the age of forty can probably name more rappers than they can doctors, lawyers or even presidents. What was once supposed to have an expiration date, is now used to peddle everything from sneakers to soft drinks.

---

[5] Pinn.

It would be an insult to label hip-hop as just music. Those that are entrenched in it know it is a lifestyle and an outlet to give a voice to the voiceless.

On the surface level, in New York City during the late 1960s and early 1970s it was all about disco music. But underneath the fur coats, satin dresses and posh nightclubs, something was bubbling.

The Bronx was on fire…literally. In just five years from 1969 to 1974, the city lost over 500,000 manufacturing jobs, which resulted in over one million households being dependent on welfare by 1975.[6] There was arson, crime, drugs, gang activity, police brutality and urban flight. Out of all that upheaval hip-hop was conceived. Most R&B singers were birthed out of the church. Most rappers were birthed out of the struggle.

These are the breaks.

Kool Herc, who by default is given credit as founder, was not simply playing records. He was playing the break on the record. The break on a record is when all the instruments drop out leaving the drums and/or bass. What made this so special? He extended the break, giving the song brand new life. That is essentially what hip-hop was and is, taking something that existed previously and transforming it into a completely

---

[6] Alec, "1970s New York Was an Absolutely Terrifying Place: 41 Photos," All That's Interesting, April 16, 2016, https://allthatsinteresting.com/1970s-new-york-photos.

different life form. Sugar Hill Gang's *Rapper's Delight* is essentially just the bass line from Chic's *Good Times*. This same idea of recreating and restructuring previously existing songs (sampling) would later cause problems once rappers began generating more profits on the new creation than the original artist did.

The individuals dancing in the middle of the party with all the people surrounding them, later become known as break dancers, because you guessed it, they danced during the break.

The one playing host to the party with a microphone in their hand would later take on the designation, master of ceremonies, or MC.

The Zulu Nation, organized by Afrika Bambaataa, was comprised of former gang members and drug dealers that were looking for another option in life. This composition of people with different skill sets, desires and interests gave rise to the culture of hip-hop, which included rapping, DJing, graffiti and break dancing. Hip-hop culture can therefore be heard and seen through four metonyms that relate the artist to the accoutrements used to craft his art: Man and mat, man and machine, man and marker, and man and microphone.[7]

The term "hip-hop" has roots that stretch back to at least the 1950s, when teen dance parties were called "hip hops" or "hippity hops," particularly by disapproving parents. The name

---

[7] Miller, Freeman and Pinn.

20

stuck, and the South Bronx parties where modern DJing and rapping were invented were called "hip hops."[8]

Stringing words together that rhymed was nothing new. This is something that was already being done by the likes of Muhammad Ali and radio personalities Hank Spann and Frankie Crocker and even in many church quartet groups. It was the marriage of the rhymes with the beat that birthed hip-hop into what it is today.

Hip-hop is part biography, part rebellion, part social commentary, and part stuntin'. It is about more than music. In fact, it transcends music. Hip-hop to many, myself included, is about the culture.

Culture is defined as the sum of attitudes, customs, and beliefs that distinguishes one group of people from another. It is transmitted, through language, material objects, ritual, institutions, and art, from one generation to the next.[9]

Because there is no hierarchy in hip-hop, there is no direct chain of command to direct the culture. The closest thing that exists are influencers, and even they change every couple of years. The culture is ever evolving, which also makes it

---

[8] Genius, "Song Lyrics & Knowledge: Rapper's Delight," Genius, accessed July 13, 2022, https://genius.com/annotations/20596/standalone_embed?dark=1.

[9] E. D. Hirsch, William G. Rowland, and Michael Stanford, *The New First Dictionary of Cultural Literacy: What Your Child Needs to Know* (Boston, MA: Houghton Mifflin, 2004).

potentially dangerous. I once heard leadership guru and strategist, Dr. Samuel Chand, say in reference to culture, "It is created at the top, sustained from the bottom, but destroyed from the middle." Hip-hop has no one person as its spokesperson. In the words of KRS-One, "I am hip-hop."

Throughout the decades, I have watched hip-hop shift from sequined outfits to Adidas tracksuits to oversized gold chains to oversized throwback jerseys to skinny jeans back to oversized gold chains. It went from vinyl albums to cassettes to "the purple tape" (yes, it gets a classification of its own) to CDs to mp3s to streaming services. It went from rapping about selling drugs to rapping about using drugs. This is all a part of the culture of which I subscribe to. The good, the bad and the ugly. Hip-hop is no longer relegated to the confines of urban America. It is global. Hip-hop has positioned itself as one of the most vital cultural forces to be reckoned with globally.[10]

In 2000, I had the opportunity to travel overseas during my undergraduate studies in graphic design to St. Gallen, Switzerland for four months. Within a week I was able to discover a hip-hop clothing store and record store in the area, where I began to split my time during my stay. I would converse with the locals in broken Swiss-German and then go listen to OutKast's *Stankonia*. I became a bit of a celebrity because not only was I an American, I was a *black* American. And in their eyes, I could only be one of two things: a ball player or, you

---

[10] Miller, Freeman and Pinn.

guessed it, a rapper. And when they discovered I wasn't either one, the next assumption was, I knew one personally. I'm not going to say I used this to my advantage, but I used this to my advantage.

This speech is my recital.

In listening to hip-hop, I have heard some of the most vile and violent words in my life. And to be honest, I loved every part of it. It makes you both cringe and bob your head at the same time. There is something infectious about the music and the culture that draws people in from all across the globe. From the Swiss Alps to the Allegheny Mountains.

Hip-hop is extremely ubiquitous. But many couldn't imagine the impact it would have on the world at large. There is not an industry or a part of the world that has not been touched or affected by it since its inception. There is no other genre of music that can make that claim. Hip-hop is more than rap music – it is an African diasporic phenomenon.[11]

Hip-hop gave a voice to young, black, urban America. Hip-hop is Allen Iverson in braids. It's making words rhyme that have no business rhyming. It's gold chains. It's gold teeth. It's wearing one pant leg up. It's a Yankee fitted. It's the Fab Five (Jalen, Juwan, Chris, Jimmy and Ray) in oversized shorts. It's Jordan's on people who don't play a lick of basketball. It's a

---

[11] Erika Gault and Travis Harris, eds., *Beyond Christian Hip Hop: A Move toward Christians and Hip Hop* (London; New York: Routledge, Taylor et Francis Group, 2021).

Dickie's outfit on people not going to work. It's being fluid when the mainstream thinks it has defined it and properly portrayed it (e.g. stopping the dab once parents and politicians started dabbing). It's Nike Cortez and Adidas Shell toes. It's creating a new vernacular. It's as much three white, Jewish guys from New York as it is two black, "city girls" from Miami.

There is a bond between hip-hop and religion that is rarely discussed. We'll discuss the deeper ties a little later. To begin, both have prophets. Think more God's mouthpiece than fortune-telling.

Whether it's Isaiah or Jeremiah, Malcolm X or Martin Luther King, Tupac or Nipsey Hussle. The prophets of old were sent by God to tell of what was to come and to speak "truth to power" regardless of repercussions.

Both have a written script that they subscribe to. In Christianity, it's the Bible. In Islam, it's the Quran. In hip-hop, it's *The Source*! *The Source* was literally coined "The Hip-Hop Bible." It is where you found information on your favorite rapper. Dissecting verses in the monthly "Hip-Hop Quotable," was like reading passages from Psalms.

These same scripts have passages that you cull about to fit the moment or the circumstance. There are bible verses related to decision-making. Verses for love. Verses for grief.

In most churches, the 23rd Psalm is the go-to standard for funeral passages for loved ones to glean from in time of mourning and reflection.

> The Lord is my shepherd; I shall not want.
> 2 He maketh me to lie down in green pastures: he leadeth me beside the still waters.
> 3 He restoreth my soul: he leadeth me in the paths of righteousness for his name's sake.
> 4 Yea, though I walk through the valley of the shadow of death, I will fear no evil: for thou art with me; thy rod and thy staff they comfort me.
> 5 Thou preparest a table before me in the presence of mine enemies: thou anointest my head with oil; my cup runneth over.
> 6 Surely goodness and mercy shall follow me all the days of my life: and I will dwell in the house of the Lord for ever.[12]

If there were a similar accumulation of words in hip-hop, it would be found in Pete Rock and C.L. Smooth's *They Reminisce Over You (T.R.O.Y.)*, which incidentally, I plan on having played at my funeral.

> I reminisce for a spell, or shall I say think back
> Twenty-two years ago to keep it on track
> The birth of a child on the 8th of October
> A toast, but my granddaddy came sober
> Countin' all the fingers and the toes

---

[12] Psa. 23 (KJV)

Now I suppose you hope the little black boy grows[13]

Honorable mentions would go to Puffy's *I'll Be Missing You*, Master P's *Is There a Heaven for a Gangsta*, Tupac's *I Ain't Mad At Cha* and Wiz Khalifa's *See You Again* (I actually eulogized a funeral where this was played).

To further examine the comparisons of hip-hop to faith, we cannot overlook the fact that both have dedicated followers. Some may refer to them as fans, or even Eminem coined, "Stans." However, the Bible calls them disciples.

A fan can be considered an enthusiastic admirer. They are the person that paints their hair and chest at sporting events, but are never in the game. They will never take a foul or get tackled. Nothing is really required of them. There is no sacrifice.

Discipleship is a little different. Discipleship in its simplest form is duplication or replication. It is where you try to take on the identity and personality of someone else to the best of your ability.

What we call Christianity was in actuality a sect/spinoff of Judaism. Before they were known as Christians at Antioch, they were called "followers of the way." It was understood, a

---

[13] Pete Rock and C.L. Smooth, "*They Reminisce Over You (T.R.O.Y.)*"

Christian is not someone who comes to church on Sunday, but somebody who lives their life the way Jesus did.

The man we claim to follow, on this mission we claim to be on, living this life that we say we're about, was hung on a cross, spat upon, mocked, and imprisoned for His revolutionary and incendiary speech.

Part of the reward for a Christian lie in how many disciples one is able to make during their lifetime. It is a part of our biblical mandate: *"Go and make disciples..."*[14].

From the start, God's design has been for every single disciple of Jesus to make disciples who make disciples who make disciples until the gospel spreads to all peoples.

While most people of faith intentionally attempt to disciple others, rappers tend to do it unintentionally. If you have ever witnessed an individual walk, talk, and dress like their favorite artist, they have been discipled. They "follow" them on social media. They believe everything they say. They tend to act out on what they hear. They are willing to argue, fight and sometimes kill in their name.

This brings up the argument as to whether rappers are responsible for their words and the influence they carry.

It is not uncommon to hear a rapper claim to "birth" a style. Part of the reason why hip-hop never died is because it

---

[14] Matt. 28:19 (NASB)

continued having children. And just like churches, you are only as strong as your youth department.

Unsolicited name drops: Shout out to Grandmaster Flash, The Furious Five, The Cold Crush Brothers, Kurtis Blow, Grandmaster Caz, Sylvia Robinson, Russell Simmons and Eddie Cheeba

NEW GOD FLOW.1

When we hug these mics we get busy
Come and have a good time with G-O-D

Ghostface Killah, *Mighty Healthy*[1]

There's an age-old argument in hip-hop regarding who is the top lyricist/artist in the game. Whether it be top five DOA (dead or alive), top ten or top fifty. From Jay Z claiming Biggie, Nas and himself. To Nas claiming Pac, Big and himself. To Dylan literally just claiming himself.

Due to the passion of the conversationalists, the topic has been known to spawn civil wars amongst family members and brawls in barbershops.

The argument is never-ending because the generational, cultural, and demographical taste is continuously evolving. The same could be said regarding basketball. Michael Jordan will forever top my list, while older generations could easily point to the fact that Bill Russell has more championship rings than he

---

[1] Ghostface Killah and Mathematics, "*Mighty Healthy*", released February 2000, track 9 on *Supreme Clientele*, Epic/Sony/Razor Sharp, https://genius.com/Ghostface-killah-mighty-healthy-lyrics.

29

does fingers. Millennials equate Jordan to gym shoes, or at the very least, the Wizards, so their basketball hero may be Lebron or KD.

When naming top MC, someone who was born in the mid-1970s may include Melle Mel or Grandmaster Caz in their all-time list. While someone born in the late 1970s, or early 1980s, may say Rakim, LL Cool J or KRS-One deserve top honors. Later generations may say a variety of people from Lil Wayne to Lil B deserve to be in the conversation, lest we leave out Kendrick, J. Cole or Drake. Someone from the East Coast has a rightful difference of opinion in saying Kool G Rap is top MC. However, someone from the Midwest will quickly bring up Eminem. Residents of the South may inject Scarface or Andre 3000 into the debate, while those on the West Coast can say Ice Cube, E-40 or maybe even MC Hammer (insert shoulder shrug emoji). Side note: I personally don't think Hammer gets enough credit.

Everyone looks for the coveted title of G.O.A.T. (Greatest of All Time) or "God MC," yet where does this idea of being God MC come from?

Whether realized or recognized, God has always had a place in hip-hop. References to God or faith has permeated rap lyrics since its inception. Run D.M.C. went from *Raising Hell* to being *Down with the King*. And Run is now known as Rev Run. Kanye went from *Jesus Walks* to *Dark Twisted Fantasies* back to *Jesus is King*. Ma$e went from *Harlem World* to pastoring, and denouncing rap altogether, to riding with 50 Cent, back to pastoring. And everyone knows being signed to Bad Boy Records can push anybody to somebody's God (insert Loon, Craig Mack, Shyne). Just kidding Puff!

I revolve around sciences.

According to a 2015 study, Christians are the largest religious group in the world today, making up nearly a third (31 percent) of Earth's 7.3 billion population[2]. But with that being said, Christianity does not have the longest standing relationship with hip-hop, nor the strongest ties. Islam is the official religion of hip-hop.[3]

New York City is the undisputed birthplace of hip-hop, and is oftentimes referred to as the Mecca, as in Islam's holiest city and the "cradle of Islam."[4] I've never heard of Sedgwick Avenue referred to as Jerusalem, Bethlehem, nor Nazareth.

The Honorable Minister Louis Farrakhan, of the Nation of Islam, has hosted hip-hop summits on both the East and the West Coasts, mediated beef between Ice Cube and Common,

---

[2] https://www.pewresearch.org/fact-tank/2017/04/05/christians-remain-worlds-largest-religious-group-but-they-are-declining-in-europe/

[3] Monica R. Miller, Anthony B. Pinn, and H. Samy Alim, "Re-Inventing Islam with Unique Modern Tones: Muslim Hip Hop Artists as Verbal Mujahidin," in *The Hip Hop and Religion Reader* (New York, NY: Routledge, 2015), p. 187.

[4] Reynold A. Nicholson, *Literary History of the Arabs* (London: Routledge, 2013), p. 62.

spoke at Nipsey Hussle's funeral and met with everyone from the trill OG Bun B to the Migos. I'm not sure T.D. Jakes can add that to his resume.

Before DMX was asking God to give him a sign, individuals such as Rakim (one-half of the pioneering duo, Eric B. & Rakim), Big Daddy Kane and X-Clan introduced the world to phrases such as, "dropping science," "knowledge of self," and "word is bond."

Many rappers and members of the Hip Hop Nation will readily admit that though they are not registered members of the Nation of Islam or self-identified members of the Five Percent Nation, they have been influenced by both in very significant ways.[5]

The Nation of Gods and Earths, also known as the Five Percent Nation, a splinter group of the Nation of Islam founded by Clarence 13 X, is built on the premise that 85 percent of the population lack "knowledge of self," while ten percent of the population have said knowledge — that the Black man is God — and hide it from the larger group. The remaining five percent are the "poor, righteous teachers" who work to spread that truth.

> 1. Who are the 85 percent? The uncivilized people; poison animal eaters; slaves from

[5] Ashahed M. Muhammad, "God's Influence In HipHop," The Final Call, July 22, 2014, http://www.finalcall.com/artman/publish/National_News_2/article_101629.shtml.

mental death and power; people who do not know who the Living God is, or their origin in this world and who worship that direction but are hard to lead in the right direction.

2. Who are the 10 percent? The rich slave-makers of the poor, who teach the poor lies to believe: that the Almighty, True and Living God is a spook and cannot be seen by the physical eye; otherwise known as the bloodsuckers of the poor.

3. Who are the 5 percent? They are the poor righteous teachers who do not believe in the teachings of the 10 percent and are all-wise and know who the Living God is and teach that the Living God is the Son of Man, the Supreme Being, or the Black Man of Asia, and teach Freedom, Justice and Equality to all the human family of the planet Earth; otherwise known as the civilized people, also as Muslims and Muslim Sons. [6]

Jews, Christians and Muslims teach that God and man are separate. The Nation of Islam, under the direction of Elijah Muhammad and now, Louis Farrakhan, teach financial independence, pride in self and race and that Master Fard Muhammad is God, or Allah, and African-Americans are God's chosen people — the original people of the planet Earth. However, Clarence 13 X, also known as Allah the Father, a former Nation of Islam member and student of Malcolm X,

---

[6] Felicia M. Miyakawa, *Five Percenter Rap: God Hop's Music, Message, and Black Muslim Mission* (Bloomington, IN: Indiana University Press, 2005), p.28.

believed that the black man and God were one and the same. He taught that the world was once known as Asia, and that because the black man is the original man, his proper title is the Asiatic black man – Father of civilization and God of the universe. Men are symbolic to the Sun and Women are symbolic to the Earth.[7]

Where did these teachings originate? You guessed it, New York City. The hometown of Busta Rhymes and Digable Planets. The Harlem based movement became extremely attractive to impoverished youth and flourished greatly on the streets and in the prisons of the tri-state area. While the movement remained primarily on the East, its impact became global.

By the late 1980s, hip-hop wasn't so much about who had the best rhymes and biggest gold chain, as much as it was about knowledge reigning supreme over nearly everyone (did you see what I did there?). This superseded the rise of gangsta music on the west coast. At this time, it was more difficult to find a rapper who wasn't influenced by the Gods and Earths than one who was.

Groups such as Brand Nubian, Wu-Tang Clan, and more currently, Jay Electronica, have overtly provided "lessons" in their rhymes and visually embodied their beliefs in videos. It was preaching on a beat and was mainstream. A belief system

---

[7] Jay Quan, "The 5 Percent Nation's Impact on Hip-Hop's Golden Era," Rock the Bells, 2022, https://rockthebells.com/articles/a-history-of-the-5-percent-nation-the-golden-era-of-hip-hop/.

became an integral part of hip-hop culture. Imagine me in elementary school with a high-top fade and an African medallion, quoting Chuck D. Public Enemy's *Fight the Power* is still my national anthem!

Ashahed M. Muhammad shares, "The old gospel songs about Moses asking Pharaoh to 'let my people go' and the deliverance of a suffering people seeking redemption are not Jewish melodies, but Black freedom songs, so it is fitting that Hip Hop would be the musical vehicle as modern day gospel songs to the youth, carrying forth these important truths and newly discovered realities."[8]

The Five Percent influence is woven into the fabric of hip-hop...literally. Rakim blatantly wears a seven and a crescent, or the universal flag, on his *Follow the Leader* album cover (credit Dapper Dan).

The foundational lessons of the Zulu Nation, the spiritual core of early hip-hop, were directly derived from the Supreme Mathematics and Alphabets. A cipher is known as a circle of MCs going back and forth with their lyrics, but it was adopted from "building in the cipher," the practice of Gods and Earths forming a circle around a speaker "dropping science" (another

---

[8] A. Muhammad.

term adopted by hip-hop), elaborating on the teachings of Supreme Mathematics and the 120 Lessons.[9]

Two aspects which characterize the Five Percenters are the Science of Supreme Mathematics and the Supreme Alphabet, both of which assign special meanings for the digits zero to nine and the A–Z alphabet. Numerical sequences, isolated letters, and/or the pairings of letters or digits with their corresponding meanings may therefore denote the presence of Five Percent Nation ideology.[10]

1 = Knowledge
2 = Wisdom
3 = Understanding
4 = Culture of Freedom
5 = Power of Refinement
6 = Equality
7 = God
8 = Build-Destroy
9 = Born

---

[9] ionehiphopwiredstaff, "The Gods of Hip-Hop: A Reflection on the Five Percenter Influence on Rap Music & Culture," Hip Hop Wired, March 24, 2010, https://hiphopwired.com/32991/the-gods-of-hip-hop-a-reflection-on-the-five-percenter-influence-on-rap-music-culture/.

[10] Christian Baker, "Enter the Five Percent: How Wu-Tang Clan's Debut Album Maps the Complex Doctrine of the Five Percent Nation," Center for the Humanities (Washington University in St. Louis Arts and Sciences, May 13, 2020), https://humanities.wustl.edu/news/enter-five-percent-how-wu-tang-clan%E2%80%99s-debut-album-maps-complex-doctrine-five-percent-nation.

0 = Cipher[11]

My original senior high school quote was taken from Method Man's *Mr. Sandman*, "Peace to the number seven. Everybody else get the four nine three eleven." Peace to the Gods (G is the seventh letter made and the number seven represents God). The quote didn't stand because I had to later explain what the alphabet equivalent of four, nine, three, eleven stood for (once again, insert shoulder shrug emoji).

It's yours, nobody else's.

Christian imagery, at least overtly, in hip-hop doesn't come along until much later and is brought to the forefront symbolically and given referential treatment by the likes of Tupac Shakur who would be portrayed on a crucifix on his album cover for his 1996 album *The Don Killuminati: The 7 Day Theory*. Nas, who has "God's Son" tattooed across his stomach, would later create controversy by reenacting Christ's march to Golgotha for his video, *Hate Me Now*.

Jay Z is often referred to as "Jay Hovah," or Hov, a shortened version of Jehovah. Kanye West, who gained popularity amongst Christian circles because of his song *Jesus Walks*, would later refer to himself as "Yeezus." Remy Ma would release a mixtape, *Shesus Khryst*, with an image of herself on a crucifix. And Game would utilize a bandana donned Christ

---

[11] Miyakawa, 26.

for his album, *Jesus Piece*. And lest we forget the Based God, Big Baby Jesus, 6 God and Ugly God.

Over the last few years, hip-hop has seen more and more rappers profess their faith on projects that have gone platinum and charted at the top of Billboard for weeks. In similar fashion as Rakim, for whom the term "God MC" originated, artists such as Kendrick Lamar and Chance the Rapper have garnered acclaim due to their bold stances regarding faith and not only displaying them on just one song, but rather throughout their projects.

Then there are individuals like Andy Mineo, Dee-1 and Lecrae, that many would categorize as Christian rap, who have garnered crossover appeal, and are having their songs played alongside artists that would be labeled as, "secular" or "worldly." However, all of the aforementioned Christian artists would readily profess that their influences came from the same secular source. Your favorite Christian rapper's favorite rapper is probably not a Christian. How is that for irony?

What's interesting to point out, early rap pioneers, and some current, that subscribed to and implemented "God Body" lyrics into their music were not labeled a sub-genre of hip-hop. It was just hip-hop. However, to openly profess Christ…and rap, places you in a separate category. We'll dig into this later.

As hip-hop grew, due in part to music videos, so did its universal reach. *Rock Dis Funky Joint* was my joint! And as much as I love Rakim Allah and Big Daddy Kane, it's hard to say anybody had a larger impact in bridging Five Percent teachings and hip-hop than the Wu-Tang Clan.

In 1993, Wu-Tang's *Enter The Wu-Tang (36 Chambers)* provided a glimpse into this complex connection between religiosity and criminal association, as they interspersed references to violence and illicit substance use between the album's glimpses of deeper Five Percent Nation principles.[12]

I slipped from African medallions and putting up a peace sign to Clarks and throwing up the "W." Side note: I had a knock-off pair of Clarks in high school because I couldn't afford the originals. I bought myself a pair of genuine Wallabees a few years ago to help heal the wound.

Wu-Tang rapped about their day-to-day living and allowed the world to peek in from the periphery. To this day, I don't know half of what Ghostface was rapping about, but he's still one of my favorites! Second side note: I still wonder how his career would have been impacted had he never taken off his mask and kept his anonymity.

While not perfect in their approach, the Killa Bees would catch some flak for how they demonstrated their affinity for the Nation, due in part for "promoting an image that associates Five

---

[12] Baker.

39

Percenters with drugs, alcohol, crime, and the objectification of women."[13]

While Five Percenters "reject association with the religion of Islam" and "describe their value system as a culture, not a religion," a "way of life" embodied in daily living, the current prominence of Christianity rests upon the previous inclusions of Islam and the Five Percent Nation more specifically.[14]

It has been over 25 years since *Enter the Wu-Tang* debuted, and while there are strong branches to the Wu family tree, "God body" talk is no longer as prevalent on the airwaves. Why is that? Regardless of religious affiliation or belief, isn't it more beneficial to hear that you are an extension of God, than not?

What, you tryna kick knowledge?

Apart from the dissemination of Five Percenter ideologies, this time period also provided a balance of social consciousness, self-identity and awareness to issues locally as

---

[13] Michael Muhammad Knight, *The Five Percenters: Islam, Hip Hop and the Gods of New York* (Oxford: Oneworld, 2009), p. 182.

[14] Baker.

well as across the globe. I still know certain African countries because of Stetsasonic's *Free South Africa*[15].

A-F-R-I-C-A
Angola
Soweto
Zimbabwe
Tanzania
Zambia
Mozambique
And Botswana
So let us speak about the motherland

I also became aware of who, then-Governor, Evan Mecham, was (he refused to recognize Martin Luther King's birthday as a national holiday) and what was occurring in Arizona at the time, by way of Public Enemy's *By The Time I Get to Arizona*. This was not information they provided in my history class or on our local news station. According to Sister Souljah, "hip-hop is a blessing because the <u>Poor</u> Righteous Teachers, Brand Nubian and KRS-One have actually been the educational system for Black kids, in place of the so-called educational system that is entirely financed by the American

---

[15] Stetsasonic, "*Free South Africa (The Remix)*", released February 1991, track 17 on *Blood Sweat & No Tears*, Tommy Boy/Warner Bros. Records, https://genius.com/Stetsasonic-free-south-africa-the-remix-lyrics.

government. And in the absence of the voice of young people in hip-hop, we would have even more chaos than we have today."[16]

Dr. Wesley Muhammad further substantiates this thought by stating, "There is no other element in the Black community that has the power to shape and direct Black culture—and through that Black life— like the rappers do."[17]

KRS-One, D-Nice, and Ms. Melodie of Boogie Down Productions; Daddy-O, Wise, Delight, and Frukwan of Stetsasonic; Chuck D and Flavor Flav of Public Enemy; Doug E. Fresh, Heavy D, Just-Ice, MC Lyte, and Kool Moe Dee came together collectively to record *Self Destruction* as a part of the Stop the Violence Movement started by KRS-One and journalist, Nelson George.[18] This would later spawn over to the West Coast where they had their own respective list of representatives under the name, The West Coast All-Stars, record *We're All in the Same Gang*.

---

[16] Anthony B. Pinn, *Noise and Spirit: The Religious and Spiritual Sensibilities of Rap Music* (New York, NY: New York University Press, 2003).

[17] A. Muhammad.

[18] Dart Adams, "How Stop the Violence Movement's 'Self Destruction' Became One of the Most Important Rap Releases," Okayplayer, August 11, 2020, https://www.okayplayer.com/music/the-making-krs-one-stop-the-violence-movements-self-destruction-single-89.html.

However, a willingness to talk about issues affecting inner-city Blacks and Latinos came at a price. According to Hip Hop historian Davey D, socially-conscience rappers faced the same systematic attacks on their message as did leaders of the civil rights and Black Power movements.[19]

Chuck D predicted Hip Hop's transformation in his 1990 classic single, *Welcome to The Terrordome.*

> When the '90s were coming in, a whole bunch of different things were happening in society that rap music was answering to, which showed itself as being a diverse art form," he recalled. "Therefore, the threat of black people having something to say, with their large vocabularies through rap music, was something that kind of threw the media on its side for a minute. So I saw this coming. As a result, the culture lost more than it gained.[20]

Once hip-hop began to go mainstream, corporations saw an opportunity and they pounced on it. Economics will always trump empowerment. It is interesting to note, the larger hip-hop grew, the further away from God it got.

---

[19] Cinque Muhammad, "What Happened to Hip Hop's Social Consciousness?," Austin Weekly News, February 10, 2021, https://www.austinweeklynews.com/2008/07/09/what-happened-to-hip-hops-social-consciousness/.

[20] C. Muhammad.

Unsolicited name drops: Shout out to Just-Ice, Gang Starr, Big Daddy Kane, Erykah Badu, The RZA, the GZA, Ol' Dirty Bastard, Inspectah Deck, Raekwon the Chef, U-God, Ghostface Killah and the M-E-T-H-O-D Man

FOLLOW THE LEADER

We are advertisements for agony and pain
We exploit the youth; we tell them to join a gang
We tell them dope stories, introduce them to the game

Killer Mike, *Reagan[1]*

No one expected hip-hop to grow to the extent that it did. It went from Ice Cube declaring he would never have dinner with the president, to Jay Z helping to campaign for the president, to Kanye running for president. It went from a "voice crying out in the wilderness," to simply being THE voice. It is hard to ignore its impact and its ascendancy on the world.

Steve Stoute paints the picture as such in his book, *The Tanning of America: How Hip-Hop Created a Culture That Rewrote the Rules of the New Economy*,

> But the tale I'm here to tell is less about the music itself and more about the atomic reaction it created, a catalytic force majeure that went

---

[1] Killer Mike, *"Reagan"*, released May 2012, track 6 on *R.A.P. Music*, Williams Street, https://genius.com/Killer-mike-reagan-lyrics.

beyond musical boundaries and into the psyche of young America - blurring cultural and demographic lines so permanently that it laid the foundation for transformation I have dubbed "tanning". Hip-hop had come in a time, in places, and through multiple, innovative means that enabled it to level the playing field like no other movement of pop culture, allowing for a cultural exchange between all comers, groups of kids who were black, white, Hispanic, Asian, you name it. Somehow the homegrown music resonated across racial and socioeconomic lines and provided a cultural connection based on common experiences and values, and in turn revealed a generationally shared mental complexion.[2]

Hip-hop represents a multi-billion-dollar industry that influences everything from automotive design and fashion to prime-time television programming, collegiate and professional sports, mass media marketing, and Madison Avenue advertising.[3]

I witnessed hip-hop duo, Tag Team, do a commercial for car insurance. What does hip-hop have to do with car insurance? Absolutely nothing! Except for the fact that they were

---

[2] Steve Stoute and Mim Eichler Rivas, *The Tanning of America: How Hip-Hop Created a Culture That Rewrote the Rules of the New Economy* (New York, NY: Gotham Books, 2012).

[3] Carl S. Taylor and Virgil Taylor, "Rap Music Provides a Realistic View of Life," in *Popular Culture: Opposing Viewpoints*, ed. John Woodward (Detroit, MI: Thomson/Gale, 2005).

performing an iteration of their song, *Whoomp! There It Is*, which came out in 1993. While I may have been in the eighth grade in 1993, I am old enough to purchase car insurance now.

Diamond, et al point out how we got to this place...

A survey conducted with male youth offenders (aged 17 to 21) of diverse ethnicities found that their musical preference was rap. The study also found that 72% of these youth believed that music influenced the way that they feel at least some of the time; however, only 4% perceived a connection between music listening and their deviant behavior.... Youth who chose to listen to rock and rap music with defiant messages were more likely to exhibit trait rebelliousness, disinhibition, and hostility using standard psychometric measures...

Most studies cannot determine whether the media shapes people's attitudes or whether people's attitudes shape their media consumption. These studies, however lend support to the argument that media content and audiences' attitudes, beliefs, and behaviors tend to be mutually reinforcing. More specifically, they show that there is a close, but not necessarily causal, link between popular music preferences and youth attitudes and behavior around drugs. As social cognitive theory predicts that the impact of music is most likely greatest when the messages are reinforced by peers and are reflects in other media. [4]

I grew up lower middle class. That means we had a house, but we didn't always have money for bills. It means my parents made too much money to be eligible for financial assistance, but not enough money to keep the lights on consistently. While I was born in the late seventies, I came of age during the "golden era" of hip-hop. To give some perspective, most of my favorite rappers are now grandparents.

Depending on who you ask, the golden era ranges roughly from the late 1980s to the mid 1990s. There were strong themes of Afrocentrism and political militancy, while the music was experimental and the sampling, eclectic.[5] Writer William Jelani Cobb says, "what made the era they inaugurated worthy of the term golden was the sheer number of stylistic innovations that came into existence...in these golden years, a critical mass of mic prodigies were literally creating themselves and their art form at the same time."[6]

[4] Sarah Diamond, Rey Bermudez, and Jean Schensul, "What's The Rap about Ecstasy?," *Journal of Adolescent Research* 21, no. 3 (2006): pp. 269-298, https://doi.org/10.1177/0743558406287398.

[5] Mandalit Del Barco, "Breakdancing, Present at the Creation," NPR, October 14, 2002, https://news.npr.org/programs/morning/features/patc/breakdancing/index.html.

[6] Jelani Cobb, *To the Break of Dawn: A Freestyle on the Hip Hop Aesthetic* (New York, NY: New York University Press, 2008), p.47.

This is the time period in which a No. 2 pencil was both a writing instrument and a life saver when it came to a cassette tape.

Where hip-hop in the late 1970s was about overcoming poverty and violence, there was an air of confidence in the 1980s. Hip-hop was now a business. What was originally considered a fad had now become lucrative and was producing household names.

Comedian, Tony Rock describes the timeline of hip-hop as follows:

I'm cooler than you (late 1970s)
I'm richer than you (early 1980s)
I'm blacker than you (early 1990s)
I'm harder than you (mid 1990s)
I'm a dealer (late 1990s)
I'm a user (present)[7]

While some can argue many of the messages were all present at the onset, the difference now is the audience and the lack of balance. Back then, for every 2 Live Crew, there was an X-Clan. Where there was a N.W.A., there was also an Arrested Development.

To those that grew up listening to hip-hop, there are certain lyrics to certain songs that resonate in your life when you

---

[7] Tony Rock, Charlie Mack, & D-Dot | Drink Champs (Full Episode), YouTube (Revolt TV, 2018), https://www.youtube.com/watch?v=tiDvgH8yNhg.

hear them marry the accompanying beat. They are instructions to your central nervous system to let every part of your body know, IT'S. ABOUT. TO. GO. DOWN! Whether it be in the house, in the car, or at the gym, you are no longer in control of your shoulders, feet and neck.

Universally, one example would be Wonder Mike kicking things off with,

> I said a hip hop the hippie the hippie
> To the hip hip hop and you don't stop
> The rock it to the bang bang boogie
> Say up jump the boogie to the rhythm of the boogie, the beat[8]

I personally brace myself whenever I hear *"Right about now, you're about to be possessed by the sounds of emcee Rob Base and D.J. E-Z Rock. Hit it!"*[9]

And you are sure to see a stampede of women anytime you hear Juvenile make the announcement that *"Cash Money Records taking over for the '99 & the 2000."*[10]

---

[8] Sugarhill Gang et al., *"Rapper's Delight"*, released September 1979, track 6 on *Sugarhill Gang*, Rhino Entertainment Company/Sugarhill Records Inc./Sugarhill Records, https://genius.com/Sugarhill-gang-rappers-delight-lyrics.

[9] Rob Base and DJ E-Z Rock, *"It Takes Two"*, released August 1988, track 1 on *It Takes Two*, Profile Records, https://genius.com/Rob-base-and-dj-e-z-rock-it-takes-two-lyrics.

[10] Juvenile, Mannie Fresh and Lil' Wayne, *"Back That Azz Up"*, released November 1998, track 13 on *400 Degreez*, Universal Recordings

An honorable mention would have to be given to the "bwok bwok, chicken chicken" at the beginning of Project Pat's *Chickenhead*, the Notorious B.I.G.'s wake up page on *Warning*, Chuck D screaming, *"1989!"[11]* on *Fight the Power* and Becky's friend that introduces Sir Mix-a-Lot's *Baby Got Back* by declaring, *"Oh, my, god, Becky, look at her butt."* After their conversation, you then get sucked into *"I like big butts and I cannot lie."[12]*

Even reading the lyrics probably made you go in for about four bars before continuing on to the next paragraph.

Hip-hop, you the love of my life.

Sanaa Lathan, in her role as Sidney Shaw, asks a pivotal question in the movie, *Brown Sugar*, "When did you fall in love with hip-hop?"[13]

For me, it was imitating three Jewish guys from New York, in the form of the Beastie Boys, by rapping line-for-line

---

and Cash Money Records, https://genius.com/Juvenile-back-that-azz-up-lyrics.

[11] Public Enemy, et al., *"Fight the Power"*, released June 1989, track 20 on *Fear of a Black Planet*, Def Jam Recordings, https://genius.com/Public-enemy-fight-the-power-lyrics.

[12] Sir Mix-a-Lot and Amylia Dorsey-Rivas, *"Baby Got Back"*, released February 1992, track 3 on *Mack Daddy*, Def American/Reprise, https://genius.com/Sir-mix-a-lot-baby-got-back-lyrics.

[13] *Brown Sugar*, directed by Rick Famuyiwa (2002; Fox Searchlight Pictures 2003), 1hr., 49 mins., DVD.

their *Licensed to Ill* album. Yes, I was all three members. I didn't have enough group mates in my neighborhood.

I remember Run-DMC coming to Cincinnati, and not being allowed to go to the concert with my brother and his friends because I was "too young." To add insult to injury, I vividly recall seeing a guy at church with a Run-DMC fedora following that. It had the logo inside and everything! As you can see, I'm still harboring resentment towards my parents for their actions.

I remember being in elementary school, sitting in my friend's brother's car listening to Ice T's *Girls L.G.B.N.A.F.* for the first time (insert mind blown emoji).

I was first introduced to Eightball and MJG in Mobile, Alabama while visiting family. I hopped in the car with one of my cousins and he popped *On the Outside Looking In* into the cassette deck. It changed my teenage mind from that moment forward.

I remember the day Pac died (in between classes during my senior year of high school). I remember the day B.I.G. died (unfortunately, still senior year of high school, six months later).

I remember the day XXXTentacion died (unknowingly clicked on an uncensored video of him slumped over in his vehicle). I remember the day Nipsey Hussle died (at a wedding reception).

I remember being in the barbershop one day around junior high, and while awaiting my turn, someone handing me Nelson George's book, *Buppies, B-boys, Baps, And Bohos: Notes On Post-soul Black Culture*. In the book, George mentions, "In each city where rap's appeal has been expanded there have been key figures who've fought authorities, peer pressure, and local inferiority complexes." [14] I am a product of that regional influence and impact.

I was born and raised in Cincinnati, Ohio. For those that have never been, Cincinnati is a traditional, conservative city in southern Ohio with roots to the underground railroad, as well as German ancestry. It has oftentimes been attributed to Mark Twain the idea, "When the end of the world comes, I want to be in Cincinnati because it's always twenty years behind the times."

While Cincinnati may not be the epicenter of hip-hop, we do fall into its cross-section. Cincinnati is possibly the most northern, southern city you will ever encounter. But technically being in the Midwest, we draw influences from all over.

We were a conscious city when Cincinnati native, Hi-Tek, connected with Talib Kweli and Mos Def. We were underground when Scribble Jam hosted a battle between a then unknown, Eminem, and MC Juice. When our I-71 counterparts Bone Thugs-N-Harmony came on the scene, everyone in the city

---

[14] Nelson George, *Buppies, B-Boys, BAPS, and Bohos: Notes on Post-Soul Black Culture* (Cambridge, MA: Da Capo Press, 2001), p.81.

was trying to rap fast and harmonize. And let's not forget, Cam'ron used to *Get It in Ohio*.

Because Cincinnati was not on the forefront of what was happening in the world, I would sit in front of my television waiting for some stranger to call into *The Box* video channel to request the latest 2 Live Crew and Sir Mix-A-Lot videos. I'm pretty sure I prayed for those videos to be played. Who answered those twelve-year-old prayers is up for discussion.

I watched *Yo! MTV Raps* religiously (pun intended). And then *Rap City* came on the scene. I would switch the television back and forth between the two to see who was showing something I had not seen before. All the while, trying to record on my VCR for later playback. I'm not sure if this is a good place to admit that I've watched a few *BET Uncut* videos. Just a few.

Fab Five Freddy, Ed Lover, Doctor Dre, Big Lez, Big Tigger, "The Mayor" Chris Thomas and Joe Clair were my tour guides.

In reference to *Yo!*, Chuck D called it "the Black CNN," recognizing it as a rare space on television for black Americans to share their perspectives.[15]

---

[15] Scott Beggs, "10 Fab Facts about 'Yo! MTV Raps'," Mental Floss, May 2, 2022, https://www.mentalfloss.com/article/553165/facts-about-yo-mtv-raps.

In a classic case of when keeping it real goes wrong, my first cousin is Fredro Starr of Onyx and Moesha fame. When their debut album came out, I was über-excited to see one of our own who made it. I remember being in my basement blasting *Throw Ya Gunz* as loud as the stereo allowed and rapping every verse at a raucous level. That is until my mom came home earlier than expected to hear me vying to be the fifth member of Onyx. Did I mention, I also shaved my head around this time because of them? What's funny, I did it back then based on choice. I do it now based on necessity.

Before I was shaving my hair off, I was begging my mom to use a hot comb to lengthen my stingy hi-top, so I could be more like Kid from Kid 'N Play, and less like Steve Urkel from *Family Matters*.

And around that same time I also had three cuts in my eye brow "tryin' to wild out,"[16] like Big Daddy Kane.

Hip-hop still bleeds out of me in everything I do...including church. To wear Jordan's and a T-Shirt in service is not a ruse or a gimmick to attract young people, it is part of who I am authentically from day-to-day. While I do it from time to time, to wear a suit every Sunday would be disingenuous.

---

[16] Jay-Z et al., *"Do It Again (Put Ya Hands Up)"*, released December 1999, track 3 on *Vol. 3...Life and Times of S. Carter*, Def Jam Recordings and Roc-A-Fella Records, https://genius.com/Jay-z-do-it-again-put-ya-hands-up-lyrics.

Many of my sermons are takes on rap songs, themes or albums. I have preached a Christology series called, *Walk This Way*, a faith series called, *Reasonable Doubt*, a mental health series called, *My Mind's Playing Tricks on Me*, and a family series called, *Naughty by Nature*, to name a few.

When individuals get baptized at our church they receive their standard baptism certificate, but they also receive a T-shirt that says BRN AGN (Born Again) in the style of the Run-DMC logo. Our church used to create a "mixtape" for first time visitors. It was a compilation of sermon clips over current hip-hop instrumentals.

I do this because I draw parallels, and am admittedly influenced, from both worlds.

While the common maxim is, all rappers want to be ball players, and all ball players want to be rappers, I believe all rappers want to be preachers, and all preachers want to be rappers.

Both deliver messages. Both create disciples. Both constantly put out new material. Both are sought after to use their platforms to sway an audience to a particular cause.

I even liken preaching to composing a rap song. There is an intro, a bridge, a climax and an outro. Word play, metaphors, and punchlines are often involved. Both feed off the response of the crowd.

Drug dealing music, hey I influence.

According to the National Institute on Media and the Family, Teens consider musicians heroes more often than athletes and rate the influence of music higher than religion or books. Music has long been a staple of kids' media diet, being the media of choice for many adolescents, frequently edging out television. Many teens use music to shape their cultural identity and to help define their social group. Some social groups are identified primarily by their choice of music.[17]

Influence is defined as the act or power of producing an effect without apparent exertion of force or direct exercise of command.[18] Influence is the ability to make somebody do something on his or her own accord.

There are three components of social influence. They are: conformity, compliance and obedience. Social influence refers to the ways people influence the beliefs, feelings, and behaviors of others.

Conformity is a type of social influence in which individuals change their attitudes or behavior in order to adhere to existing social norms. Conformity is generally regarded as a passive form of influence in that members of the group do not

---

[17] Fact Sheet. National Institute on Media and the Family. 3 July 2001. 6 August 2007

[18] Merriam-Webster dictionaries s.v. "influence (*n.*)", accessed, July 25, 2022, https://www.merriam-webster.com/dictionary/influence.

actively attempt to influence others. People merely observe the actions of group members and adjust their behaviors and/or views accordingly.

Compliance is a form of social influence involving a direct request from one person to another.

Obedience is defined as a form of social influence in which one person obeys direct orders from another to perform some action(s). In compliance, you have some choice. In obedience, you believe that there is no choice.

In life, we tend to either be the influencer or the influenced. To say hip-hop, and its artists, has a direct influence on everything we do is an understatement.

For the longest, I thought I was supposed to grind until I couldn't anymore, because Nas taught me that "sleep is the cousin of death."[19] To his defense, I also was not big on wasting money on short-term pleasures, because "that buck that bought a bottle could've struck the lotto."[20]

---

[19] Nas and DJ Premier, *"N.Y. State of Mind"*, released April 1994, track 2 on *Illmatic*, Sony Music Entertainment, https://genius.com/Nas-ny-state-of-mind-lyrics.

[20] Nas et al., *"Life's a Bitch"*, released April 1994, track 3 on *Illmatic*, Sony Music Entertainment, https://genius.com/Nas-lifes-a-bitch-lyrics.

If you asked me my preference in women when I was younger, I would have told you, "I like 'em brown, yellow, Puerto Rican or Haitian."[21]

Run D.M.C. had an entire generation wearing Adidas. Nelly had another generation wearing Nike Air Force Ones.

As Steve Stoute puts it, hip-hop created a "dog-whistle effect in the frontal lobes of youth everywhere. Ghetto and barrio kids would hear the stories of trailer parks and get it. Kids in affluent homes or in sleepy suburbs heard the call of generational despair and understood it. The commonality no longer had to be shared experience per se, but was about the linkage of feelings—all kinds of emotions that could be conjured by a thumping beat, rhymes, wordplay, anger, humor, arousal, resentment, boredom, joy, excitement, curiosity, you name it."[22]

This also has its down side. Statistically, only black rappers get gunned down. No other genre of music or culture is that violent. Juveniles are now thinking being a drug dealer and/or gang member is cool because their favorite rapper makes

---

[21] A Tribe Called Quest, *"Electric Relaxation"*, released November 1993, track 8 on *Midnight Marauders*, Zomba Recording Corporation, https://genius.com/A-tribe-called-quest-electric-relaxation-lyrics.

[22] Stoute and Rivas, p. 33.

it look cool. Some of them are middle class kids who have never missed a meal but want to be gangstas.

Hip-hop is one of the United States' biggest exports.[23] But what makes exposure dangerous is when there's too much of it.

Throughout time music has used its influence as a tool, both knowingly and unknowingly. Marvin Gaye's *Let's Get It On* and Teddy Pendergrass' *Turn Off the Lights* are labeled "baby making" music because they suggest certain acts. So, it's no coincidence that when two adults prepare to have consensual sex, they throw on one of these songs, or something similar, because the lyrics and the melodies help to change the mood or set the atmosphere.

Gospel music icon, Yolanda Adams, did not make the playlist when it came to the conception of my two children. I would go out on a limb and dare to say Yolanda Adams was not on Yolanda Adam's playlist during the conception of her own children.

The Bible tells us, *"faith comes from hearing"*[24]. So, in laymen's terms, the more that I hear a particular thing, the more I believe in it.

---

[23] Beggs.

[24] Rom. 10:17 (NASB)

The tangible effects don't take place until one makes a conscience decision to move upon that which was heard. If *Faneto* or *Down For My N****z* gets played at a venue and violence breaks out, it's not necessarily Chief Keef's or C-Murder's lyrics that are completely to blame. The individuals involved have deeper issues that need to be addressed. The music just placed suggestions as to where, or how, to direct their inner angst.

Why do you think many athletes play their favorite songs before a big game? They want to hype themselves up. It activates the amygdala, which is the section of the brain that processes emotions. Corianne Rogalsky, an assistant professor of speech and hearing science at Arizona State University, said, "When the amygdala is active it increases our ability to consolidate memories, which is why when we hear that emotional song before the big game…you sort of trigger emotionally that part of your brain."[25]

They're not planning on going out and mowing down thirty people with a semi-automatic weapon. They are allowing themselves to be charged for battle. It just so happens that their battle is taking place on a different turf.

---

[25] Nicholas White, "Music Does More than Hype Athletes, It Helps Prep the Brain for Action," Global Sport Matters, November 25, 2019, https://globalsportmatters.com/health/2019/11/25/music-does-more-than-hype-athletes-it-helps-prep-the-brain-for-action/.

From the word influence we also get influenza, which many understand to be the common flu. Typically, influenza is transmitted from infected individuals through the air by coughs or sneezes. This means that it is transferable. The virus takes shape and abides within a host subject that is susceptible to sickness or has a weakened immune system. Vaccinations against influenza are usually given to people in developed countries with a high risk of contracting the disease.

Just as with coughing, I am able to transfer my influence upon somebody else by not monitoring my mouth. If a person isn't on guard, they can easily be infected. Most physicians would concur when I say, high potency + close proximity = high impact.[26]

Unsolicited name drops: Five Deez, Mood, Mr. Dibbs, Jibri the Wise One, OTR Clique and K-Riley.

---

[26] Bill Hybels and Mark Mittelberg, *Becoming a Contagious Christian* (Grand Rapids, MI: Zondervan, 2007).

D'EVILS

There's a war going on outside no man is safe from
You can run but you can't hide forever

Prodigy (Mobb Deep), *Survival of the Fittest*[1]

Music is everywhere around us. Whether in commercials, during sporting events or in worship services. Music is played while waiting on hold for customer service to answer questions regarding charges to your account. In fact, there is no point in time in which music has not been present. No matter the time period, the culture or the style, some form of musical arrangement has made the journey. So, it becomes hard to separate faith and spirituality from music, because music is as old as life itself.

One of the earliest references to music is via a descendant of Cain. I refer to Cain as Killa Cain (both as a reference to the movies *Menace II Society* and *Paid in Full*, because Caine was one of the main antagonists in the former and

---

[1] Mobb Deep, *"Survival of the Fittest,"* released April 1995, track 3 on *The Infamous,* BMG Music, https://genius.com/Mobb-deep-survival-of-the-fittest-lyrics.

Killa Cam would go on to kill his "brother" Mitch in the latter—sorry, that's just how my brain works).

> 17 Cain made love to his wife, and she became pregnant and gave birth to Enoch. Cain was then building a city, and he named it after his son Enoch. 18 To Enoch was born Irad, and Irad was the father of Mehujael, and Mehujael was the father of Methushael, and Methushael was the father of Lamech.
>
> 19 Lamech married two women, one named Adah and the other Zillah. 20 Adah gave birth to Jabal; he was the father of those who live in tents and raise livestock. 21 His brother's name was Jubal; he was the father of all who play stringed instruments and pipes.[2]

This particular passage introduces us to an individual by the name of Jubal. Jubal is oftentimes credited as the starting point or the "father" of music. But what's a father without children? From Jubal, music begins to be incorporated in all types of festivals, celebrations and worship.

There is mention of tambourines and dancing in Exodus as Moses and the children of Israel celebrate their escape from Egypt across the Red Sea[3]. Joshua and his troops used ram's horns as trumpets to bring down the walls of Jericho[4]. Then there

---

[2] Gen. 4:17-21 (NIV)

[3] Ex. 15:20 (NLT)

[4] Josh. 6 (NASB)

is the story of King Jehosophat who was spending his time sending out troops trying to convince people why they should serve his God. In doing so, he developed enemies. His enemies joined together to come against him in battle. In the midst of war, he appointed his singers to go out first[5].

King David ushers in the golden era of music. David is a psalmist. He is a song writer. With every crisis in his life, he writes a song about it. He's part Chris Brown, part Bobby Brown, part Drake. He's both sensitive and a little ratchet. He is the original bad boy of R&G (rhythm and gospel).

Saul, who is David's predecessor, is borderline bipolar and deals with mood swings and terrible bouts of depression. His people tell him about David, who is then subsequently hired to play his harp to help soothe his spirit[6].

At the height of temple worship, they had choirs, shofars (ram's horn), cymbals, tambourines and various other instruments being integrated. Historian, Irene Hesk, notes that of the thirty-nine books of the Old Testament, the 150 Psalms ascribed to King David, have served as "the bedrock of Judeo-Christian hymnology," concluding that "no other poetry has been set to music more often in Western civilization."[7]

---

[5] 2 Chron. 20:21 (NLT)

[6] 1 Sam. 16:14-23 (NASB)

[7] Irene Heskes, *Passport to Jewish Music: Its History, Traditions and Culture* (Milwaukee, WI: Hal Leonard, 2002), p.41.

John the Baptist, who was the forerunner to Jesus, was beheaded due to music...indirectly. You see, John criticized King Herod for divorcing his wife and marrying his sister-in-law, Herodias, who was married to his brother, Philip. His punishment for speaking out was imprisonment, but that wasn't satisfactory enough for Herodias. Herodias had a daughter, Salome, who performed a birthday dance for Herod so well that he made a vow to give her whatever she desired, up to half his kingdom[8]. Her request, via her mother, was John's head on a platter. Now, I don't know what kind of dance would cause a man to risk it all (it has been labeled as "the dance of the seven veils"), but I'm going to venture to say, it wasn't ballet.

It's bigger than hip hop.

For the sake of simplicity, we thus far have labeled hip-hop as a genre of music. But in actuality there is only one classification of music...worship. That is what music's original intent was, to worship God. Before there was earth, there was heaven. The current soundtrack of heaven is worship. Contrary to popular opinion, there is no Biggie, Tupac, Nipsey cipher happening in heaven right now with Jam Master Jay providing the beat.

Part of the job description for angels was and is worshipping God. There was an angel who was in charge of

---

[8] Mark 6:23 (NASB)

leading all of the other angels in worship. We know him by many names, but the primary one is Satan.

Satan, whose home was heaven, would eventually be cast out. What was Satan's crime? Satan was guilty of arrogance. Believing he had equal billing as God.

The Bible teaches that Satan is in no way equal with God. He is a created being. His origins begin as an angel. And what was his occupation? Musician.

Some say minister of music. Others say worship leader. Either way, he was the man. So much so, he had a built-in studio. His origins point back to the Old Testament book of Ezekiel:

> 13 "You were in Eden, the garden of God; Every precious stone was your covering: The ruby, the topaz and the diamond; The beryl, the onyx and the jasper; The lapis lazuli, the turquoise and the emerald; And the gold, the workmanship of your settings and sockets, Was in you. On the day that you were created They were prepared. 14 "You were the anointed cherub who covers, And I placed you there. You were on the holy mountain of God; You walked in the midst of the stones of fire. 15 "You were blameless in your ways From the day you were created Until unrighteousness was found in you."[9]

---

[9] Ezek. 28:13-15 (NASB)

Great care must be taken when interpreting this particular passage. While some of the phrases in Ezekiel describe the king of Tyre, some also describe the devil. It becomes evident that at times in this chapter the author is describing this king in terms that could not be applied to a mere human. This king had been in the Garden of Eden[10], had been anointed as a guardian cherub[11], and had access to the holy mountain of God[12], but was driven from there[13].

This description in the King James Version makes mention of "the workmanship of thy tabrets and of thy pipes," which describes the curious music he had, the tabrets and pipes, or hand instruments and wind instruments.

In a pivotal scene from the movie, *The Usual Suspects*, Kevin Spacey, who plays "Verbal" is describing a mysterious figure that goes by the name, Keyser Söze.

> Nobody ever believed he was real. Nobody ever knew him or saw anybody that ever worked directly for him, but to hear Kobayashi tell it, anybody could have worked for Söze. You never knew. That was his power. The greatest

---

[10] Ezek. 28:13 (NASB)

[11] Ezek. 28:14 (NASB)

[12] Ezek. 28:14 (NASB)

[13] Ezek. 28:16-17 (NASB)

trick the Devil ever pulled was convincing the world he didn't exist.[14]

You cannot believe in Jesus and not believe in the devil, because Jesus believed in the devil. He is not to be feared, but he is to be respected. He's mentioned in Genesis. He's mentioned in Revelation. Jesus mentions him throughout the gospels. And while some may choose to ignore him, it doesn't mean you're not being impacted by him. Just because something is invisible doesn't mean it's insignificant. We can't see germs, but living through a pandemic, many of us wouldn't readily allow someone to cough on us.

In Paul's letter to the church of Ephesus, he encourages them to "Put on the full armor of God, so that you will be able to stand firm against the schemes of the devil"[15]. He tells the church of Corinth something similar when he says "For we are familiar with his evil schemes"[16].

How does the devil wage war against us? Primarily through his schemes. These are his tactics, strategies and methods. Your adversary knows he cannot overpower you. He can only outplay you, or better yet, in the words of DJ Khaled, make you "play yourself."

---

[14] *The Usual Suspects*, directed by Bryan Singer (1995; Gramercy Pictures 2002), 1hr., 46 mins., DVD.

[15] Eph. 6:11 (NASB)

[16] 2 Cor. 2:11 (NASB)

Renowned boxing trainer Cus D'Amato once said, "To see a man beaten not by a better opponent, but by himself is a tragedy."

We first see the devil's schemes in Genesis as he deals with Adam and Eve. He showed up in the garden, not with a red jumpsuit and horns, but as a snake. If you've ever had a garden, you're not surprised to see snakes there. When he shows up, he acts like he belongs where he is.

So how do we become aware of his schemes? His schemes are revealed in his names.

Hi, my name is.

He comes in many forms, but it is the same agenda.

Many know him as Satan. That name means adversary. He is our enemy. He opposes God's agenda. He's a blocker. He wants to block everything that's good.

Another common name is Devil, which means slanderer. 1 Peter 5:8 tells us, "Be of sober spirit, be on the alert. Your adversary, the devil, prowls around like a roaring lion, seeking someone to devour."

When you are not sober your discernment, or awareness, is off. When your guard is down, you'll settle for something you ordinarily wouldn't have.

Lucifer means shining one. This means he's not going to come to you ugly and scary, chasing you with a pitchfork. This is why Jesus tells us to watch AND pray. Just because I cannot see the trap, doesn't mean there isn't one. Everything that looks good, isn't good. Let me use the prophetic voice of TLC to remind you, "Don't go chasing waterfalls. Stick to the rivers and the streams that you're used to."[17]

For the purposes of this book, the name for Satan I wanted to get to is, the prince of this world, or the "god of this world"[18]. The New Testament book, Ephesians, further calls him the "prince of the power of the air"[19].

Music is transmitted via air waves. You see where I am going with this? Sound consists of waves transmitted through the air (or another substance) by molecules bumping into each other. When these sound waves reach your ear, they cause your ear drums to vibrate. Your brain "decodes" the vibrations into voices, music, and noises.[20]

---

[17] Lisa "Left Eye" Lopes, et al., *"Waterfalls"*, released November 1994, track 8 on *CrazySexyCool*, LaFace Records and Arista Records, https://genius.com/Tlc-waterfalls-lyrics.

[18] 2 Cor. 4:4 (NASB)

[19] Eph. 2:2 (NASB)

[20] National Space and Air Museum, "Waves in the Air," How Things Fly, accessed July 24, 2022, https://howthingsfly.si.edu/aerodynamics/waves-air.

Luke 10 describes a war that takes place in heaven, in which the devil found himself on the losing end of. Because Satan tried to rebel against God, He had to be punished. Part of his sentence was to be cast out of the palatial estates of Heaven. God casts Satan out of Heaven, along with a third of the angels. But, if he got cast out, where did he go? Here's a clue. It wasn't hell.

This is why bad stuff happens to good people. Why funeral homes and news stations will never go out of business. Why there is murder, molestation and mayhem throughout the world. And why certain behaviors are allowed and even promoted. We are fighting a fight on the enemy's turf.

While many will recognize his final resting place to be in hell, they fail to realize where he ends up in the meantime…here on earth.

You done learned a lot from Satan.

Despite recent events, *The Cosby Show* ranks as one of the greatest television shows that allowed minorities to see themselves in a different light. Not to mention, Theo, played by Malcolm-Jamal Warner, was so hip-hop!

Outside of when the Huxtables celebrated Cliff's parents' anniversary by performing Ray Charles' *Night Time Is the Right Time* (Keshia Knight Pulliam killed that!), there is one episode that has always been a favorite of mine, and that's "A Shirt Story."

In this particular episode, fourteen-year-old Theo brings home a $95 Gordon Gartrell shirt (named after a writer and producer on the show). After discovering the price, his father forces him to return the designer garment back to the store. Observing his plight, his sister, Denise, offers to make him a knock off version of the shirt that ultimately doesn't come out quite right. Hilarity ensues. Cue credits.[21]

The moral of the story, no matter how much you try, a counterfeit can never compare to the original. But based on the findings (counterfeit and pirated products amounted to as much as $509 billion in 2016[22]), it doesn't stop people from getting fooled.

Best-selling book, *The Art of War* by Sun Tzu, has become an increasingly popular reference book for several decades for everything from investing in the stock market to managing corporate mergers and buyouts. At its heart, it is a

---

[21] "The Cosby Show," *A Shirt Story* (New York, NY: NBC, October 18, 1984).

[22] Danny Grajales Perez-y-Soto, "Counterfeiting and Piracy in 2021 – the Global Impact," Anti-counterfeiting and Online Brand Enforcement: Global Guide 2021 - World Trademark Review, May 11, 2021, https://www.worldtrademarkreview.com/global-guide/anti-counterfeiting-and-online-brand-enforcement/2021/article/counterfeiting-and-piracy-in-2021-the-global-impact.

manual of wisdom on handling conflict of any kind. In it, Sun Tzu proclaims, "All warfare is based on deception."[23]

The devil is a deceiver. The Bible calls him the father of lies[24]. Unfortunately, we are extensions of his family tree. As Dr. Dharius Daniels puts it,

> Our world in general, and this nation in particular, is fascinated with fantasy. We buy houses we can't afford, fraternize with people we don't like, and attend parties dressed in outfits we plan to return in order to be accepted by strangers who barely know our names. The success of reality TV shows that aren't depicting reality and of billion-dollar entertainment industries reveals a fatal flaw about the human condition: we are infatuated with fiction. Deception is a fiction narrative based on a true story prompted by a decision to substitute reality for idealism. In other words, we don't keep it real.[25]

The devil is not a creator. He's an imitator. He specializes in knock offs. Counterfeits. Perversions. At one time you could spot a counterfeit a mile away. Now, it takes a trained

---

[23] Sun Tzu, *The Art of War*, ed. John Minford (New York, NY: Penguin Books, 2002).

[24] John 8:44 (NASB)

[25] Dharius Daniels, *Represent Jesus: Rethink Your Version of Christianity and Become More like Christ* (Lake Mary, FL: Passio, 2014), p. 53.

eye to spot a fake. The devil is not the biggest threat or enemy of the church—ignorance is.

The devil is a hater who doesn't have any original ideas, so he takes God's stuff and perverts it. Pornography is roughly a $97 billion dollar industry globally, of which the United States makes up $10-$12 billion of that[26]. When you take into account the pandemic, Pornhub, one of the world's biggest XXX websites, reported increases ranging from 38% to 61% -- well above its astonishing 2019 average of 115 million unique visits per day (42 billion annually)[27]. If you watch(ed) porn you're not going to hell...I don't think...and I hope not...for my friend's sake. However, the devil did not create sex. He is not that smart.

Pornography raises men's expectation of how women should look and changes men's expectations of how women should behave. Not that I've ever engaged in said activity, but nobody gets interrupted by their kids in porn. Everybody's house is clean. And apparently nobody cooks or gets hungry.

There is only one devil. He is not God. He is not omnipresent. Most of the time we're not dealing with the devil.

---

[26] CNBC.com, "Things Are Looking up in America's Porn Industry," NBCNews.com (NBCUniversal News Group, January 20, 2015), https://www.nbcnews.com/business/business-news/things-are-looking-americas-porn-industry-n289431.

[27] Nick Tate, "Porn Use Spiked during the Pandemic," WebMD, May 26, 2021, https://www.webmd.com/lung/news/20210526/porn-use-spiked-during-the-pandemic.

We're dealing with his employees. Just like angels work for God, demons work for Satan.

STRANDED ON DEATH ROW

I was so money orientated, initiated as a thug
Fiendin' for wicked adventures, ambitious as I was
Picture a nigga on the verge of livin' insane
I sold my soul for a chance to kick it and bang

2Pac, *Good Life*[1]

People are weird! When I say weird, I'm not talking about regionally weird (Florida Man), but more like weird as a species. We do things no other living entity does. Water spills from our eyes when we're sad, and sometimes when we're happy. We shave hair off our faces and/or bodies to deem ourselves more attractive. We take pictures of our food. After a certain age, we stop drinking the milk of our own kind and consume milk from another group. Weird, right?

On a larger scale, as people, we treat other people (of the same species) differently because they're…well, different (race, socioeconomic status, sexual preference). Not to mention, we lie.

---

[1] 2Pac, et al., *"Good Life"*, Released March 2001, Track 5 on *Until the End of Time*, Amaru Entertainment/Death Row Records and Interscope Records, https://genius.com/2pac-good-life-lyrics.

We steal. We cheat. We shoot up schools. We assassinate our heroes. No other group can boast these claims.

But why do we do it? You don't have to teach a child to lie or manipulate. They do it instinctively. I don't have to teach my children to lie. I have to teach them to tell the truth. So, are we inherently evil and thus produce evil things?

Scripture reminds us of our frailty:

For I was born a sinner—
yes, from the moment my mother conceived me.[2]

for all have sinned and fall short of the glory of God,[3]

And I know that nothing good lives in me, that is, in my sinful nature. I want to do what is right, but I can't.[4]

Even the book of Kendrick admonishes us:

I am a sinner
Who's prob'ly gonna sin again
Lord, forgive me, Lord, forgive me[5]

---

[2] Psalm 51:5 (NLT)

[3] Rom. 3:23 (NIV)

[4] Rom. 7:18 (NLT)

[5] Kendrick Lamar et al., "*Bitch Don't Kill My Vibe*", Released October 2012, Track 2 on *good kid, m.A.A.d city (Deluxe Version),* Top Dawg Entertainment/Aftermath Entertainment and Interscope Records, https:// https://genius.com/Kendrick-lamar-bitch-dont-kill-my-vibe-lyrics.

Social psychology researcher, Roy Baumeister, believes the factors driving people to do bad things to each other are highly complex. In his seminal work, *Evil: Inside Human Violence and Cruelty*, he determines "there are four major root causes of evil or reasons that people act in ways that others will perceive as evil. Ordinary, well-intentioned people may perform evil acts when under the influence of these factors, singly or in combination."[6]

1. The simple desire for material gain
2. Threatened egotism
3. Idealism
4. The pursuit of sadistic pleasure[7]

Beyond this list, others may want to include social settings, peer pressure or mental health. But, if I consider myself spiritual, I have to be aware of things I can see as well as the things I cannot see. And if you don't think you're not affected by things you cannot see, tell that to gravity.

A factor that is flippantly used, but mostly misunderstood, is demonic influence. When we want to categorize a level of evil that is logically unexplainable, we say it's "demonic." To the point, you don't have to really believe in demons to classify something as such.

---

[6] Roy F. Baumeister, *Evil: Inside Human Violence and Cruelty* (New York, NY: W.H. Freeman, 2013), p. 13.

[7] Baumeister, p.13.

When someone says demon or possession, many of us automatically think of *The Exorcist* or *Poltergeist* (which I don't fool with to this day) and heads turning, or foaming at the mouth. While there are cases of abnormal displays, demon possession is not what most of us think. It does not mean the demon has the person. It means the person has the demon. It is only when the man has a spirit that the spirit can have the man. I know what you're thinking. We stepped into the spooky chapter. But, bear with me for a couple pages.

Let's get one thing out of the way, if I believe in the presence of the Holy Spirit in my life, then I cannot be demon possessed! If I believe God dwells in me, then that's like saying, God can be evicted by the devil.

But, while I cannot be possessed, I can be oppressed, afflicted and tormented to different degrees by demonic powers.

There are varying degrees of satanic influence. And just because my head is not spinning 360 degrees does not mean I'm not suffering from any type of demonic activity.

At the core of demonic possession is a person under the power or influence of a demon(s). So, what is a demon?

If you believe in angels, then you have to believe in demons. Just like angels work for God, demons work for Satan. A demon is a fallen angel. They have a standing reservation in hell. But, until their reservation date, where do they operate? You guessed it, on Earth.

In the Bible, Peter makes an analogy between the Devil and lions. He gives a stern warning to, *Be sober, be vigilant; because your adversary the devil walks about like a roaring lion, seeking whom he may devour.*[8]

The lion is considered the king of the jungle. The roaring lion is the male lion. And his roar is one of the loudest noises any animal on Earth can make. It can be heard from miles away.

The male lion has the roar, but the one you need to be afraid of is the lioness. The lioness doesn't roar, she bites. Traditionally, she is the one that does the hunting. When the lioness brings down the prey, then the lion comes to get the food.

Your adversary roars, but he lets other folk do the dirty work while he stands back and watches.

There is only one devil, but there are many demons. And while we don't reside in the same house, they do live in my neighborhood. You have the Holy Spirit and spirits. They're fighting for the same thing—influence.

'Cause it's not safe for you.

In his classic sermon entitled, *Watch Them Dogs*, Rev. B.W. Smith tells the story of a man with a small dog that lived next door to a man with a big dog. Every morning the owner of the big dog would walk his dog past the house of the small dog. The small dog would hop off the porch and cause a bunch of

---

[8] 1 Pet. 5:8 (NKJV)

commotion and make a lot of noise by barking at the big dog and running into the gate knowing his master had locked it.

One day the owner of the small dog forgot to lock the gate. When the owner of the big dog came walking his dog past the house, the small dog went into his regular pattern of annoyance by running into the gate. This time the gate flew open. As you can imagine, the big dog took advantage of this surprising opportunity and tore into the small dog. When the beating was finally over, the small dog retreated to his alcove and asked the quintessential question, "Who in the hell left the gate open?"

As a society and a nation supposedly founded on Godly principles, we have drifted further and further away from God. Dare I say, some of the results we've been getting is because we've left the gate open. I can allow a bad spirit to jump on me by leaving the gate open too long.

I was watching cable one day and noticed how words like f***k and b***h and n**** were freely allowed to be used. This is a far cry from when I used to sneak to watch Cinemax when my parents were sleep (don't judge me). The difference now is, all of this is on basic cable!

I remember the backlash Nelly received when he swiped a credit card between the butt cheeks of a young lady in *Tip Drill*. Or back when they showed a bare buttock on *NYPD Blue*. Now, this is standard practice.

The Federal Communications Commission (FCC) is the federal agency responsible for implementing and enforcing America's communications law and regulations.[9] They are the gatekeepers for everything we see and hear via radio, television, wire, satellite, and cable in all 50 states. And before they existed, there was the Hays Code.

The Hays Code dictated what was and wasn't acceptable from movies to television.

In 1927 they came up with a list of things that couldn't appear in movies:[10]

1. Pointed profanity—by either title or lip—this includes the words God, Lord, Jesus, Christ (unless they be used reverently in connection with proper religious ceremonies), Hell, S.O.B., damn, Gawd, and every other profane and vulgar expression however it may be spelled;
2. Any licentious or suggestive nudity—in fact or in silhouette; and any lecherous or licentious notice thereof by other characters in the picture;
3. The illegal traffic in drugs;
4. Any inference of sex perversion;

---

[9] "About the FCC," Federal Communications Commission, accessed December 5, 2022, https://www.fcc.gov/about/overview.

[10] MPPDA Digital Archive, *"Magna Charta"*, Resolution, Record #365, frames 3-2396 to 3-2419, from MPPDA Digital Archive, Flinders University Library Special Collections, https://mppda.flinders.edu.au/records/365 (assessed July 14, 2020).

5. White slavery;
6. Miscegenation;
7. Sex hygiene and venereal diseases;
8. Scenes of actual childbirth—in fact or in silhouette;
9. Children's sex organs;
10. Ridicule of the clergy;
11. Willful offense to any nation, race or creed; and

BE IT FURTHER RESOLVED, that special care be exercised in the manner in which the following subjects are treated, to the end that vulgarity and suggestiveness may be eliminated and that good taste may be emphasized:

1. The use of the Flag;
2. International Relations (avoid picturizing in an unfavorable light another country's religion, history, institutions, prominent people and citizenry);
3. Arson;
4. The use of firearms;
5. Theft, robbery, safe-cracking, and dynamiting of trains, mines, buildings, et cetera (having in mind the effect which a too-detailed description of these may have upon the moron);
6. Brutality and possible gruesomeness;
7. Technique of committing murder by whatever method;
8. Methods of smuggling;
9. Third-Degree methods;
10. Actual hangings or electrocutions as legal punishment for crime;
11. Sympathy for criminals;

12. Attitude toward public characters and institutions;
13. Sedition;
14. Apparent cruelty to children and animals;
15. Branding of people or animals;
16. The sale of women, or of a woman selling her virtue;
17. Rape or attempted rape;
18. First-night scenes;
19. Man and woman in bed together;
20. Deliberate seduction of girls;
21. The institution of marriage;
22. Surgical operations;
23. The use of drugs;
24. Titles or scenes having to do with law enforcement or law-enforcing officers;
25. Excessive or lustful kissing, particularly when one character or the other is a "heavy".

When it came to television, couples in the same bed had to follow the one-foot rule. That meant one of them had to have at least one foot on the ground while in the bed.[11]

Of course, many of these regulations no longer exist, and/or have been modified partially due to desensitization and/or to keep up with the changing times. But what came first,

---

[11] Josh Lanier, "'The Brady Bunch': Debunking the Myth Show Was First to Feature Couple Sleeping in the Same Bed," Outsider, February 22, 2021, https://outsider.com/entertainment/brady-bunch-debunking-myth-show-first-feature-couple-sleeping-same-bed/.

the chicken or the egg? Did people change or did something change the people?

Illuminati want my mind, soul and my body.

> For we do not wrestle against flesh and blood,
> but against principalities, against powers,
> against the rulers of the darkness of this age,
> against spiritual hosts of wickedness in the
> heavenly places.[12]

There are different levels of demons. It has been suggested, the highest level of demon is principality. The concept of principalities is understood by the Greek word arche meaning chief or ruler. Principalities rule and reside over regions. Las Vegas is traditionally considered Sin City. New Orleans is the murder capital of the U.S.[13] Seattle has the least sunny days out of a majority of states in America. Which adds to its claim to the highest percentage of adults taking

---

[12] Eph. 6:12 (NKJV)

[13] Michaela Romero, "Skyrocketing Homicide Rates in 2022 in New Orleans: Murder Capital of the U.S. Report Says" (WGNO, September 20, 2022), https://wgno.com/news/louisiana/orleans-parish/skyrocketing-homicide-rates-in-2022-in-new-orleans-murder-capital-of-the-u-s-report-says/.

medications for their mental health.[14] Detroit has one of the highest poverty rates in the country.[15]

Powers deals with the warrant or right to do something, or delegated influences of control.[16] The fruits of this type of evil can probably be seen in: drug cartels, plagues, terrorism, and other heinous crimes against humanity, even toward the animal kingdom.

Satan works in people by "broadcasting" his basic attitude to the mind through different mediums, i.e. music. He is actually "on the air," so to speak, surcharging the air around the world.

God gave Satan and his demon subordinates substantial authority over everything from the earth's atmosphere on down to the earth itself, which includes us, its inhabitants. Satan is revealed as "the god of this world." We must never forget, in

---

[14] Gene Balk / FYI Guy, "Seattle Ranks as Most Medicated Metro for Mental Health Reasons," The Seattle Times (The Seattle Times Company, January 3, 2022), https://www.seattletimes.com/seattle-news/data/seattle-ranks-as-most-medicated-metro-for-mental-health-reasons/.

[15] Andrew DePietro, "U.S. Poverty Rate by City in 2021," Forbes (Forbes Magazine, November 9, 2022), https://www.forbes.com/sites/andrewdepietro/2021/11/26/us-poverty-rate-by-city-in-2021/?sh=1a1c69075a54.

[16] Robin Dinnanauth, *Call to Duty: Advanced Warfare* (Woodhaven, NY: Robin Healing Ministries, 2015), p.26.

large part, our wrestling, as Paul terms it, is with these spirits. We inhabit the same space they do.

We are not fighting rappers, or even musicians for that matter. What we are facing is SPIRITual warfare. We can never underestimate the capabilities of our adversary or the deceptiveness he will use to defeat us. Satan does not fight alone. Nor does he fight fair. So why would he not choose people of influence to carry out his deeds, in particular musicians who are able to tap into the emotions of an individual with their music and place suggestions in their minds? Maybe this is why they are called "suggestive" lyrics.

Unless you live under a rock, Rick James' 1978 hit *Mary Jane* was code for marijuana use. It was and is a smoker's anthem. While its origination was probably not intended to influence a generation of future tokers, he made it look cool and acceptable way before it was legalized.

Fast forward over thirty-five years later and Future is rapping:

> A bunch of girls goin' wild when your chain
> flooded
> And I had 'em like wow, cup dirty
> Dopeman, dopeman, dopeman, dopeman,
> dopeman, dopeman
> Money on the counter, choppers on the floor
> I just copped that tempo, DJ Mustard, woo

Way too much codeine and Adderall[17]

Future speaks of, amongst other things, his consumption of lean, which is a recreational beverage composed of codeine cough syrup, candy, and sometimes, alcohol. However, it is also an opiate similar to morphine, oxycontin or Vicodin. Codeine triggers the same brain receptors as heroin—promethazine, an antihistamine, is not advised to be mixed with alcohol.

Just as Rick James was not the spokesman for marijuana, neither is Future the sole advertiser of codeine and Adderall. However, with ninety-five million units certified[18] and thirty million followers on social media, his influence is to be documented. Prior to his accidental overdose, Juice WRLD, credited Future as his reasoning for trying "dirty Sprite" as a kid.

The Apostle Paul, in speaking to the church, writes:

19 When you follow the desires of your sinful nature, the results are very clear: sexual immorality, impurity, lustful pleasures, 20 idolatry, sorcery, hostility, quarreling, jealousy, outbursts of anger, selfish ambition, dissension,

---

[17] Metro Boomin, Future and Drake, "*Jumpman*", Released September 2015, Track 9 on *What a Time to Be Alive,* OVO Sound/Republic Records/Young Money/Freebandz/Epic Records and Cash Money Records, https://genius.com/Drake-and-future-jumpman-lyrics.

[18] Tony M. Centeno, "Future Beats Drake's Record to Become Most Platinum Rapper of 2010s," iHeart (iHeartRadio, July 28, 2022), https://www.iheart.com/content/2022-07-28-future-beats-drakes-record-to-become-most-platinum-rapper-of-2010s/.

division, 21 envy, drunkenness, wild parties, and other sins like these. Let me tell you again, as I have before, that anyone living that sort of life will not inherit the Kingdom of God.[19]

While much of his list appears to be self-explanatory, the word used for sorcery/witchcraft is actually pharmakeia, from whence we get the word pharmacy (drugs). You can make a stretch and say he was alluding to all pharmaceuticals, because while I've never done drugs, those that suffer from allergies, like myself, know Benadryl is sure to get you high.

Witchcraft at its core is manipulation. Even though he named one of his albums *The Wizrd*, Future Hndrxx isn't chief commander of the underworld. I mean, he can't be. He's connected to one of my favorite rap collectives, The Dungeon Family. Wait, that didn't help his case.

Whether it's Future, or Lil Wayne before him, the pattern is to provide individuals with fame and fortune in exchange for a platform to guide minds and shift cultures. While I don't subscribe to conspiracies, I don't believe in coincidences either.

How you gonna see him if you livin' in the fog?

Clarksdale, Mississippi is a small town just east of the Arkansas border in the Mississippi Delta. It has a population of roughly 15,000 people, but yet musicians from across the globe

---

[19] Gal. 5:19-21 (NLT)

make a pilgrimage to Coahoma County. It is the birthplace of legendary crooner, Sam Cooke. But more notably, it is the birthplace of blues musicians, John Lee Hooker, Muddy Waters and Robert Leroy Johnson.

As folklore has it, Robert Johnson was a harmonica and mediocre guitar player that aspired for more. With a desire to become a great blues musician, Johnson was instructed to take his guitar to the crossroads of Route 49 and 61 near Dockery's plantation at midnight. At the crossroads, Johnson was met by a large man, considered to be the Devil, who took the guitar from him and tuned it, ultimately giving him mastery of the guitar. The Devil proceeded to hand the guitar back to Johnson in return for his soul. In exchange, Robert Johnson became able to play, sing, and create the greatest blues anyone had ever heard.

> I went to the crossroad, fell down on my knees
> I went to the crossroad, fell down on my knees
> Asked the Lord above, "Have mercy now
> Save poor Bob if you please[20]

The once unknown, would later become the standard when it came to blues music and the grandfather of Rock 'n' Roll, influencing the likes of Keith Richards, Eric Clapton and Bob Dylan. While most of his fame is posthumous, he has sold

---

[20] Robert Johnson, *"Cross Road Blues (Take 1)"*, Released May 1937, track 17 on *The Complete Recordings*, Vocalion Records, https://genius.com/Robert-johnson-cross-road-blues-take-1-lyrics.

millions of records and his name lives in infamy as being attributed to the devil's assistance.

While some dispute the story, and even the location, that intersection has become a tourist attraction.

Several decades later Snoop Dogg would give a similar tale in the form of *Murder Was the Case*[21]:

> A voice spoke to me and it slowly started saying
> (Bring your lifestyle to me, I'll make it better)
> How long will I live? (Eternal life and forever)
> And will I be the G that I was?
> (I'll make your life better than you can imagine
> or even dreamed of
> So relax your soul, let me take control
> Close your eyes my son) my eyes are closed

Do I believe either actually sold their soul? No. Do I believe many have compromised themselves for notoriety and financial gain? Absolutely. When doing so, the enemy manipulates what gets distributed and where, to create his desired end—destruction.

Music is a strong spiritual force and the message behind the beat is absorbed on a spiritual level. Oftentimes, we're drawn

---

[21] The D.O.C., Kurupt and Daz Dillinger, *"Murder Was the Case (Death After Visualizing Eternity),* Released November 1993, Track 8 on *Doggystyle*, Death Row Records/Interscope Records and Atlantic Records, https://genius.com/Snoop-dogg-murder-was-the-case-death-after-visualizing-eternity-lyrics.

in by the music itself, the melody, the tones, the tunes, the rhythm, the chords. The ear is the birth canal to our Spirit.

Is it possible to love God and still listen to hip-hop? I know that's the question you've been reading eighty pages to have answered.

I don't think that it is necessarily evil to listen to non-Christian music, but there should be a balance. Christians are not called to be the fun police. Everything does not require our surveillance or commentary. We are called to live out our faith, not legislate it.

I do not hide from the fact that I grew up on hip-hop and it still plays a factor in my daily life. But, at the same time I'm not over consumed by everything that gets distributed. In laymen's terms, I don't eat everything that's cooked.

Many of you reading this don't participate in the office potluck at Thanksgiving because you know not all of your coworkers can cook. Not to mention, you've witnessed some of them leave the restroom without washing their hands.

"You are the salt of the earth. But what good is salt if it has lost its flavor? Can you make it salty again? It will be thrown out and trampled underfoot as worthless.[22]

You've never tasted salt that tasted like mac n cheese, but you have tasted mac n cheese that tastes like salt. Side note:

---

[22] Matt. 5:13 (NLT)

if you have to spell out the word macaroni, it probably doesn't have enough love or salt in it.

Whenever salt gets in something, salt becomes the dominant influence. God wants to pour out His children into dry, lifeless, bland places so we can have influence, not be influenced. I don't know where you work, but it should be salty tomorrow.

Be careful when you become numb to your environment. There's a problem when I'm no longer affected by misogyny, violence, sex, and drugs. It's hard to saturate your Spirit with ungodly things and expect it to work right when you need it to.

In order to maintain balance in my life I do something called intermittent fasting.

Fasting is the act of denying yourself of something that you like/want for a period of time. Some do it to lose weight. I do it to give my soul a break.

I take periodic breaks of differing lengths from social media, explicit music, movies and television shows for the purpose of regaining control. And whether the break is two weeks or two months, when/if you return to hearing or seeing those things, it becomes a shock to the system. Meaning, it typically wasn't meant to be digested regularly.

41st side south

IMA BOSS

You should do what we do, stack chips like Hebrews

Jadakiss, *It's All About the Benjamins*[1]

It is an undeniable fact that the Five Percent Nation has some of the deepest ties to hip-hop. But to disregard or ignore Jewish influence on the art form would be meshuggeneh. Not so much from being in front of the mic, which there are some (The Beastie Boys, MC Serch, Lil Dicky, Mac Miller, Drake), but from being behind the desk. Behind the success, and some may say demise, of a majority of your favorite rappers are "God's people."

One of the looming stereotypes of Jews, is their association with money. More so their handling of money. They were the first ones to be linked to the notion of "get rich or die trying."

One of the original framers of said stereotypes is Shakespeare's Shylock character from the play *The Merchant of*

---

[1] Puff Daddy, et al.,," *It's All About the Benjamins Remix"*, recorded, July 1996, track 10 on *No Way Out*, Bad Boy Entertainment and Arista Records*, https://genius.com/Diddy-its-all-about-the-benjamins-remix-lyrics*.

Venice. He is among history's best-known caricatures of the Jewish businessman. In this late 16th century play, Shylock is a Jewish moneylender who extends a loan guaranteed by a pound of flesh from the Christian merchant Antonio. When Antonio's ships are lost at sea and he cannot repay the loan, Shylock summons him to court where, despite being offered twice the original loan as repayment, he insists on exacting his pound of flesh, which he plans to obtain by lopping it off Antonio's body with a knife. [2]

Now, the name Shylock is used to describe someone who is a loan shark or someone who lends money at high rates of interest. This is what is also considered usury.

The problem with usury is it typically unfairly enriches the lender and takes advantage of the sometimes-desperate borrower. This is frowned upon in most religious circles that preach emancipation or not having anyone be a "master" over you other than God.

When Jesus chose to eat and associate himself with tax collectors, his actions were frowned upon and questioned. "Why does your teacher eat with tax collectors and sinners?"[3] Tax collectors had a reputation for being crooked agents. They were

---

[2] Joellyn Zollman, "Jewish Immigration to America: Three Waves," My Jewish Learning, May 19, 2017, https://www.myjewishlearning.com/article/jewish-immigration-to-america-three-waves/.

[3] Matt. 9:11 (NIV)

Jews who worked for the Roman government collecting taxes. They took a commission on the taxes they collected and then overcharged the people and pocketed the difference.

The tax collectors were hated and considered cheaters and traitors. On the social scale, tax collectors were at the bottom. They were barred from worshiping in the synagogue. They had no social or religious life. They had few friends.

Because "moneylending" and tax collecting were frowned upon, many early medieval Christians shied away from the industry. This left the finance industry as the only available option for a group of people that were ostracized from most professions by local rulers during the Middle Ages. It became a means of survival.

How does this tie into hip-hop? Jews eventually fled the hostile old European world and concentrated in New York and the East Coast of the United States, and later in Hollywood as well. Pushed out of Europe by overpopulation, oppressive legislation and poverty, they were pulled toward America by the prospect of financial and social advancement.[4]

In addition to settling in New York, Philadelphia, and Baltimore, groups of German-speaking Jews made their way to Cincinnati, Albany, Cleveland, Louisville, Minneapolis, St.

---

[4] Joellyn Zollman, "Jewish Immigration to America: Three Waves," My Jewish Learning, May 19, 2017, https://www.myjewishlearning.com/article/jewish-immigration-to-america-three-waves/.

Louis, New Orleans, San Francisco, and dozens of small towns across the United States. During this period there was an almost hundred-fold increase in America's Jewish population from some 3,000 in 1820 to as many as 300,000 in 1880. [5] Immigration and entrepreneurship are two central themes in the history of the Jews in the United States.[6]

From the 1880s, Jewish immigrants and their descendants built and designed the American entertainment and music industry. They opened publishing houses, ran vaudeville halls and entertainment clubs, established dominant music management companies, opened independent record labels, and controlled successful corporations.[7]

Black bar mitzvahs.

Before Rabbi Abraham Joshua Heschel and Reverend Martin Luther King Jr. marched arm-in-arm from Selma to Montgomery, Jews and African-American's lives intersected through music. According to the musical compilation exhibit,

---

[5] Irving Berlin et al., "From Haven to Home: 350 Years of Jewish Life in America a Century of Immigra-tion, 1820-1924," Library of Congress, September 9, 2004, https://www.loc.gov/exhibits/haventohome/haven-century.html.

[6] Rebecca Kobrin, *Chosen Capital: The Jewish Encounter with American Capitalism* (New Brunswick (NJ): Rutgers University Press, 2012).

[7] Ari Katorza, *Stairway to Paradise Jews, Blacks, and the American Music Revolution* (Berlin: De Gruyter Oldenbourg, 2021).

Black Sabbath: The Secret Musical History of Black–Jewish Relations,

> "in the 1930s, the song 'Eli Eli'—based on
> King David's lament in the 22nd Psalm—
> became a staple for left-leaning progressives
> like Paul Robeson and a must-cover for Black
> artists like Duke Ellington and Ethel Waters.
> For Waters, the song spoke to a history of
> shared suffering. It tells the tragic history of the
> Jews as much as one song can," she said, "and
> that history of their age-old grief and despair is
> so similar to that of my own people that I felt I
> was telling the story of my own race too."[8]

The race industry reflected the emergence of new styles in black popular music. What eventually became known as rhythm and blues evolved out of a trimmed down, ensemble-based jazz band sound synthesized with the blues music of blacks who had recently migrated from rural parts of the South to cities such as New Orleans, Houston, Memphis, New York, Detroit, Chicago, Cincinnati, and Los Angeles.[9]

The new terms "race music" and "race records" were birthed out of "black pride, militancy, and solidarity in the 1920s, and it was generally favored over colored or Negro by African-

---

[8] "Black Sabbath: The Secret Musical History of Black–Jewish Relations," The CJM, August 26, 2010, https://www.thecjm.org/exhibitions/22.

[9] Kobrin, 142.

American city dwellers," noted scholar William Barlow states in *Cashing In: 1900-1939.*[10]

When it came to telling their own stories, prior to the 1940s, African Americans were scarcely represented on radio, and live performances were largely limited to segregated venues. Race music and records, therefore, were also the primary medium for African-American musical expression during the 1920s and 1930s; an estimated 15,000 titles were released on race records—approximately 10,000 blues, 3,250 jazz, and 1,750 gospel songs were produced during those years.[11]

Jonathan Karp highlights the interaction that developed between Jews and African-Americans in the industry at that time.

> "Race" music was a term employed by the recording industry in the years 1920 to 1955 to describe commercial music made by blacks for blacks. Between 1945 and 1955 many of the most significant companies specializing in race music (or "rhythm and blues," as it later came to be known) were owned or co-owned by Jews. These were independent ("indie") labels that exploited the vacuum left by the "majors," the established music corporations, in servicing the black record market. They included such influential labels as King in Cincinnati; Savoy in

---

[10] Matthew A Killmeier, "Race Music," Encyclopedia.com (St. James Encyclopedia of Popular Culture, June 21, 2022), https://www.encyclopedia.com/media/encyclopedias-almanacs-transcripts-and-maps/race-music.

[11] Ibid.

Newark; Apollo, Old Time, and Atlantic in New York; Chess and National in Chicago; and Specialty, Aladdin, and Modern in Los Angeles, as well as many others of lesser stature and duration. The men, and occasionally women, who ran these companies were Jewish entrepreneurs, business people first and foremost, only sometimes with a previous strong interest in and deep knowledge of black music. Although the successful ones came to take the music seriously, to the point of making detailed studies of its commercial qualities, their activity was driven by money, not aesthetics. In true Adam Smithian fashion—that is, out of self-interested motives—they provided black musicians with unprecedented opportunities to record and acquire fans. But they also almost invariably exploited black artists who were doubly vulnerable: individually as musicians lacking in independent capital and collectively as members of a subordinate racial caste in a still largely segregated society.[12]

Karp further assesses, "the story of these business pioneers is a morally ambiguous one…but their Jewishness cannot be ignored; if these men and women tended to be infrequent attendees at synagogue, they nevertheless evolved a

---

[12] Chosen Capital by Jonathan Karp (Blacks, Jews, and the Business of Race Music, 1945-1955), 141.

kind of Jewish subculture" that requires recognition and analysis."[13]

Fast forward to the late seventies, early eighties and what we have is an early, fledgling form of music, in the form of hip-hop, that other major labels did not want to touch because of its newness and association with being dirty. And you now have a group of people (Jews) willing to fill a void and provide opportunities where others would not.

Much can be argued on whether it was more for an appreciation of the craft or simply financial gain, but when you look at who calls the shots in music industry, particularly hip-hop, it is hard not to see Jewish influence.

Some tall Israeli.

The vast majority of the major publishing companies in Tin Pan Alley, which at the end of the nineteenth century became the main production area of the American music industry, were owned and run by Jews. Apparently, about forty percent of the independent record labels of the post-World War Two era were owned or managed by Jews. In addition, Jews ran and controlled two of the largest and most successful record

---

[13] Kobrin, 6.

labels in the late 1960s: CBS Records and Warner Communications.[14]

Herman Lubinsky, owner and founder of Savoy Records in New Jersey, recorded jazz legends Charlie Parker and Miles Davis. Syd Nathan of King Records, in my hometown of Cincinnati, once signed, recorded and distributed a young James Brown. Brothers Phil and Leonard Chess of Chicago gave us Etta James, Howlin' Wolf and Muddy Waters. Some may say, without Rick Rubin there is no Def Jam. With no Def Jam, there is no LL Cool J, Public Enemy or Run D.M.C.. Without Rubin, there is also no production for Jay Z's *99 Problems*. Past Def Jam president, and present Global head of Music for YouTube, Lyor Cohen, is responsible for opening the door for the likes of Redman, DMX, Ja Rule and Ludacris.

It is Jimmy Iovine's Interscope Records that provides us with Tupac Shakur's debut *2Pacalypse Now*, Death Row Records' catalog (Dr. Dre, Snoop Dogg and Eminem are branches on this tree), as well as Marky Mark and the Funky Bunch. I guess Iovine could have kept that last one. Steve Rifkind, of the now defunct Loud Records (also son of Spring Records' Jules Rifkind), housed acts such as The Alkaholiks, Wu-Tang Clan, Mobb Deep, Three 6 Mafia, and Big Pun. He also helped to provide us with the cult classic, *Paid In Full*.

---

[14] Katorza, Ari. Stairway to Paradise: Jews, Blacks, and the American Music Revolution, Berlin, Boston: De Gruyter Oldenbourg, 2021.

While the aforementioned may fall under the category of "cool Jews" in hip-hop, there is a tawdry side of this fairy tale. For every Steve Rifkind there is an Art Rupe, founder of Specialty Records. This is the label that would go on to sign Little Richard. When Richard's *Tutti Frutti* broke through and began selling millions of records, his contract stated that he would only receive a fraction of the proceeds. This came about to supposedly half a cent for every copy, while white artists at that time were making ten times as much.

Labels smelled the desperation on young, poor, Black artists, and offered them lopsided record deals where the company would own their music in perpetuity.

Hip-hop trio, De La Soul, would fall victim to this unfair practice when they signed to Tom Silverman's Tommy Boy Records. This is the label that gave the world Queen Latifah, Afrika Bambaataa and Digital Underground. While the majority of artists have their music catalogs available on streaming services, De La Soul does not. This is based largely on their original contract that stated that they would only receive ten percent of the revenue generated, with the other ninety percent going to Tommy Boy. Similar stories are told of Jerry Heller (Ruthless Records), Benjy Grinberg (Rostrum) and William Socolov (Fresh). Editor's note: De La Soul's catalog is now available for streaming as of March 3, 2023 thanks to a deal with Reservoir Media, who acquired Tommy Boy Records.

Biz Markie was known to the world for his personality as well as his hit song, *Just A Friend*. While his song would go on to reach number nine on the Billboard 100, he would never see any money from the actual sales. His money, like many artists, came from touring and doing shows. And unfortunately, in his case, once you die so does that stream of income. The song will live on for decades, but it will primarily only benefit the family of the executives that drew up the contract...and *their* offspring.

Q-Tip's (A Tribe Called Quest) infamous regulatory warning, "Industry rule number 4,080: Record company people are shady,"[15] was said to be directed towards Jive Records and its founder, Clive Calder. Can you guess Clive's background?

I'm just sayin' you could do better.

While these practices were more the rule than the exception, the argument can be made that proper representation would have prevented some of these deals. But a greater conversation to be had than the contract is the content.

Hip-hop has long been criticized for its subject matter. Much of it over the years has centered on over-sexualization,

---

[15] A Tribe Called Quest, "*Check the Rhime*", released September 1991, track 9 on *The Low End Theory*, Zomba Recording Corporation, Jive Records and RCA Records, https://genius.com/A-tribe-called-quest-check-the-rhime-lyrics.

misogyny, homophobia, toxic masculinity, violence, drugs and the like.

Arguments have been made regarding its long-term effects on its consumers, which in the beginning was primarily African-American youth. BUT you can only eat what you are being fed.

When my son was a baby, we spent a lot of time in Children's Hospital. He had rickets and on top of that he was throwing up a lot. After a series of tests, we discovered he had food allergies. What we were feeding him was making him sick. So, what did we do as caring parents? We changed his diet. He would only eat what we provided him until he was old enough to recognize for himself what was and was not good for him.

Before a song gets airplay, it passes through certain industry gatekeepers. They have the opportunity to promote or shut it down. Do artists share responsibility for their content? Absolutely! They created it. But when it comes to distribution, marketing, promotion and funding, the control typically does not rest in their hands.

Whether current or past, the following Jewish executives hold/held prominent positions in a music industry that gave/gives more access to sexism and stereotypes than empowerment and education.

Len Blavatnik (Warner Music Group)
Edgar Bronfman (Warner Music Group)

Stephen F. Cooper (CEO, Warner Music Group)
Lucian Grainge (CEO, Universal Music Group)
Julie Greenwald (COO, Atlantic Records)
Stanley R Harris (XXL Magazine, King Magazine)
John Janick (CEO, Interscope Records)
David Mays and Jon Schecter (The Source Magazine)
Sumner Redstone (Viacom – BET, VH1, MTV)
Paul Rosenberg (Def Jam Records, Goliath Records)

This very short list of names used as an example can be traced to thousands of hours of music that promotes violence and degradation that is targeted to a specific group of people. While it can be argued, that this is a conversation centered on "free speech" and it is all a part of the game, the game seems to pit young African-Americans against everyone else.

I have listened to a ton of derogatory music in my day. I mean a ton! I should have been a drug dealing pimp that occasionally gets high while committing armed robberies near my subsidized housing. But in all of my musical selections, I have never heard any anti-Semitic, anti-gay, anti-white women songs make it to the mainstream, or even off the shelf for that matter. If something does happen to slip through the cracks, it's quickly shut down. I will go out on a limb and guess that distribution and promotion of songs that degrade Jewish women would look a little different.

In this age of cancel culture, you can be "canceled" for homophobic, anti-Semitic, and anti-Asian speech, but not anti-black. Twitter has a way of keeping record of an individual's derogatory statements for the sake of resurfacing in case when said individuals become famous. But it appears those statements against African-Americans are forgiven and forgotten the most.

C. Delores Tucker wasn't wrong! Now, before you shut the book, let's put this in a frame of context. While she came to notoriety for her public battles with Tupac and Interscope Records, in the late 1990s she argued that rich, White men were working to control and distort a potentially powerful and community sustaining art form turning it against the very Black communities from which it came.

While young people of all backgrounds are the targets, twelve- to eighteen-year-olds in particular, it is the agenda of a fully grown, White and mostly male elite that determines the content and popularity of what – if left unchecked – is often a highly critical, thoughtful and radical art form.[16]

Tucker purchased stock in Time Warner (Interscope parent company), which allowed her the privilege of attending shareholders' meetings and speaking out. At a May 1995 shareholders' meeting, she stood and asked the executives to read aloud the very lyrics through which their company reaped such profits. They refused.[17]

---

[16] Jared Ball, "Hip-Hop's Still Troubled Narrative: A Requiem for C. Delores Tucker," iMWiL!, June 8, 2022, https://imixwhatilike.org/2017/10/28/hip-hops-still-troubled-narrative-requiem-c-delores-tucker-jared-ball/.

[17] "C. Delores Tucker," Biography (Your Dictionary), accessed July 4, 2022, https://biography.yourdictionary.com/c-delores-tucker.

While some credited Tucker's outrage to her age, social class and not being able to relate to the current generation, when you fast forward 25 years, the concern is still the same.

This is not an attack on my Jewish brothers and sisters, but rather highlighting a glaring indictment on an industry in which they have a major influence in. To summarize, the relationship with Jews is now too enduring to forget, too disturbing to forgive, yet too intimate to dissolve.[18]

Unsolicited name drops: Shout out to Asher Roth, Action Bronson, The Alchemist, Necro, Ill Bill, DJ Drama, Vlad the Butcher, The High and Mighty and Shyne

---

[18] Kobrin, 163.

LORD KNOWS

As long as the Lord's in my life I will have no fear
I will know no pain from the light to the dark
I will show no shame, spit it right from the heart

DMX, *Lord Give Me a Sign*[1]

Of the world's largest religious groups, Christianity stands at number one. Catholicism is the largest sect of Christianity, followed by Protestantism.

On October 31st, 1517, Martin Luther wrote to Albert of Mainz, protesting against, amongst other things, the sale of indulgences. Indulgences were a way of paying priests to stay out of hell. Luther enclosed in his letter a copy of his "Disputation of Martin Luther on the Power and Efficacy of Indulgences," which came to be known as The Ninety-Five Theses.

Luther posted the Ninety-Five Theses, which he had composed in Latin, on the door of the Castle Church of

---

[1] DMX and Scott Storch, *"Lord Give Me a Sign"*, released August 2006, track 15 on *Year of the Dog...Again*, Sony BMG, https://genius.com/Dmx-lord-give-me-a-sign-lyrics.

Wittenberg.[2] Within two weeks, copies of the Theses had spread throughout Germany; within two months throughout Europe.[3] His Ninety-Five Theses was printed and circulated widely; subsequently he issued broadsheets outlining his anti-indulgences position.

The broadsheet contributed to the development of the newspaper — an advanced avenue on getting a message across quickly and effectively. He broke the internet and went viral before going viral was a thing.

In posting his Ninety-Five Theses on a German cathedral door, Luther, as Buursma pointed out, "proved that a powerful statement of faith, placed in a prominent location, can capture the attention of thousands of Christians. Even the Pope."[4]

This would spark the Reformation Movement. Reformations correct excesses of a previous movement and help evolve the church in a direction truer to Christian roots.

---

[2] Heiko A. Oberman, *Luther: Man Between God and the Devil* (New York, NY: Image Books, 1989).

[3] Walter Kramer and Gotz Trenkler, "Luther," *Lexicon Van Hardnekkige Misverstanden* (Netherlands: Bert Bakker, 1997): pp. 214-216.

[4] Bruce Buursma, "Parish Running Religion up Ad Flagpole," Chicago Tribune, August 9, 2021, https://www.chicagotribune.com/news/ct-xpm-1986-10-31-8603220090-story.html.

Luther leveraged cutting edge technology to get the Bible into the hands of the people who needed and wanted it. Luther wanted people to have the option of either reading or hearing the Bible in their own language. So, he translated it, put it through the printing press, and gave it to people in their homes. Not only did he change the way people related to God, he actually flattened the power structure of the early Church. He took the power from the "haves" (clergy) and gave it to the "have-nots" (normal, everyday Christians).[5]

There are currently over 2 billion Christians in the world. That is nearly a third of the Earth's population. Of that number, 160 million of them are Protestant Christians that reside in the United States.[6] From there, derives thousands of subsets, or denominations, by which many are associated or grouped based on doctrine and practices.

So, when someone is looking for a church, the common question asked is, "What denomination are you?"

One can choose from the Southern Baptist, the National Baptist USA, or the National Missionary Baptist. Not to be mistaken with the Progressive National Baptist, the American

---

[5] Justin Wise, *The Social Church a Theology of Digital Communication* (Chicago, IL: Moody Publish-ers, 2014).

[6] Pew Research Center, "Christian Traditions," Pew Research Center's Religion & Public Life Project, April 26, 2022, http://www.pewforum.org/2011/12/19/global-christianity-traditions/#protestant.

Baptist or the National Primitive Baptist. And let us not forget the United Methodist, the African Methodist Episcopal, the African Methodist Episcopal Zion, Assemblies of God, Church of God, Church of God in Christ or the Churches of Christ. And even though nondenominational means without a denomination, they are still grouped into a classification...or a denomination.

Out of that small list of Protestant groups, most do not associate with each other, even though they claim to exist under the larger banner of Christianity.

Similarly, hip-hop as a spoken art form has multiple sub-genres. What started as simply rap spawned into denominations such as backpack, horrorcore, hyphy, chopped and screwed, gangsta, crunk, drill, hardcore, snap, trap, underground, and not to mention, Christian/holy hip-hop.

When OutKast meets the writings of Moses.

If you are 35 years of age, or older, chances are your first introduction to hip-hop music was not via the Gospel Gangstaz.

If you asked me to name five Christian rappers when I was a teenager, let alone three, ok let's be real, I couldn't name one. I could however tell you that *Illmatic*, *Ready to Die*, *Southernplayalisticadillacmuzik*, and Common's *Resurrection* all came out in the same year (1994). How was Jesus supposed to compete with that?!

Hip-hop is both music and culture, so while I can rap about everything from injustices, police brutality, and apartheid, to pimping women, selling drugs, and using drugs, Christianity has struggled on whether to integrate or segregate.

The original notion was Christians can't be rappers, let alone listen to rap, because of its subject matter. Not to mention, according to our beliefs, we're supposed to stand out, not fit in. The bible is replete with messages of being "separate" and not "conforming." To name a few:

Do not follow the crowd in doing wrong.[7]

Oh, the joys of those who do not follow the advice of the wicked, or stand around with sinners, or join in with mockers.[8]

Don't copy the behavior and customs of this world,[9]

And we are instructed to turn from godless living and sinful pleasures. We should live in this evil world with wisdom, righteousness, and devotion to God,[10]

You adulterers! Don't you realize that friendship with the world makes you an enemy of God? I say it again: If you

---

[7] Ex. 23:2 (NIV)

[8] Psa. 1:1 (NLT)

[9] Rom. 12:2 (NLT)

[10]Titus 2:12 (NLT)

want to be a friend of the world, you make yourself an enemy of God.[11]

Do not love this world nor the things it offers you, for when you love the world, you do not have the love of the Father in you. 16 For the world offers only a craving for physical pleasure, a craving for everything we see, and pride in our achievements and possessions. These are not from the Father, but are from this world. 17 And this world is fading away, along with everything that people crave. But anyone who does what pleases God will live forever.[12]

So, to couple yourself to a genre that glorifies violence, drug use and promiscuity is hypocritical in some eyes, which makes the struggle real for those who are genuine believers, yet have this sweetest taboo.

While Christianity, Islam, and Judaism have close affiliations, Christianity has the least impact of the three when it comes to hip-hop. Due in part to the connotations associated with the art form. I like how Owen Strachan puts it, "Hip-hop had to come to church, sneaking in the back door."[13]

---

[11] James 4:4 (NLT)

[12] 1 John 2:15-17

[13] Curtis Allen and Owen Strachan, "Does God Listen to Rap?: Christians and the World's Most Controversial Music," in *Does God Listen to Rap?: Christians and the World's Most Controversial Music* (Adelphi, MD: Cruciform Press, 2013), p.7.

I haven't introduced my kids to hip-hop, formally. That is to say hip-hop is like a woman that I had a separate child by that they don't know about yet. Informally, I've been gauging their temperature to outside influences. Right now, my daughter is an early teenager and could care less. Other than the *Frozen* soundtrack when she was younger, she listens to whatever's on in the car, which is typically gospel. My son, who is a couple years older, has a different ear. While I still guard my house as much as possible from negative forces, he took to children's show, *Hip Hop Harry*, early. He's not familiar with Lil Uzi Vert yet, nor can he name the top five mainstream artists out, but he is able to recognize popular songs that become connected to video games, commercials and/or movies. One or more of the aforementioned gateways led him to an interest in Juice WRLD and Polo G.

Because I am a product of the unforeseen directions hip-hop can lead someone, I intentionally steered him in the direction of gospel rap. When we're in the car together he requests that I play something from that playlist on my phone. He recognizes a dope beat and complex rhyme patterns. He'll ask what certain metaphors mean or allude to. He has taken to NF, Lecrae, K-Drama and Social Club Misfits, amongst others.

Most of our musical discussions occur in the car while on the way to or from school or baseball practices and games. One of these days in particular, he asked to be in control of the ride soundtrack. I was prepared for him to put on some OutKast or Fugees, some This'l or maybe even someone with Lil, YBN or NBA in front of their name. Instead, he opted for pop rock band, Imagine Dragons. I'll blame that choice on his early, private school education.

On one end, I feel like I failed as a parent because he only knows Ice Cube as that guy from *Are We There Yet?* and Will Smith as the main actor on the *Fresh Prince of Bel-Air* and "that alien movie," and not simply as THE Fresh Prince.

There are moments when I will take liberties to educate. Both kids heard a snippet of Slick Rick's *Children's Story* and automatically wanted to hear more, so I obliged by putting it on repeat for a couple of days. My wife and I taught them the Humpy Dance, and they know that *Christmas in Hollis* will get played every December 25th.

One summer day, while on the way home from church incidentally, the radio was on the urban adult contemporary station (they play gospel in the morning), and *I'm Bad* by LL Cool J came on. I proceeded to roll down the windows, turn the volume all the way up and show my son I still had the breath control to go bar for bar with James Todd Smith. Yes, complete with using my hand as a "shark fin."

One sixteen to brag on my king.

Today, when you hear the phrase Christian hip-hop, one of the first names that comes to mind is Lecrae, who has done a masterful job of blurring the lines of a genre that was once considered corny to being played in your local barbershop. But before there was a Lecrae, there was Cross Movement, The Ambassador, The GRITS, who I remember seeing on Rap City once, and T-Bone.

Now, I have no beef with the early pioneers, but for those of us that were groomed on that boom bap and urban storytelling, Christian rap didn't appeal to us. I remember my best friend's mom giving him a cassette of some Christian artist (I don't think I even bothered to care of the name at the time). We promptly laughed, tossed the tape across the room and proceeded to listen to some Naughty by Nature.

While rapping about Christ gets some notoriety now, the genre actually dates back to the 1980s with artists like Stephen Wiley and Michael Peace. The first produced and commercially distributed rap album by a Christian, Stephen Wiley's *Bible Break* (1985), is also the first instance of an entity using the term "Christian Rap."[14]

A lot can be said as to why Wiley and Peace, as well as others that followed their path, didn't break through to a larger platform the same way Digable Planets or Brand Nubian did when they publicly professed their faith on their albums. It can't be because the former was too preachy in their message. Brand Nubian literally has a song called, *Allah U Akbar*. They also

---

[14] Erika Gault and Travis Harris, *Beyond Christian Hip Hop: A Move toward Christians and Hip Hop* (New York, NY: Routledge, Taylor et Francis Group, 2021).

have a song on the same album called, *Steal Ya 'ho*, but that's beside the point.

It seems as if when the lyrics are void of profanity, it automatically gets the Christian hip-hop stamp. Houston rhyme sayer, Chamillionaire, ran into this problem. When he decided to record a profanity-free album, *Ultimate Victory*, 50 Cent suggested he go sell gospel, since he was "so righteous."[15] While he identifies as Christian, which many artists do, that's just not the market he was catering to.

In 2004, when Kanye's *Jesus Walks* took the world by storm, no one in the hip-hop community considered it Christian rap, while it may have been a type and shadow to what he is doing now. But the Stellar Awards, which recognizes achievements in the gospel music industry, were quick to jump the gun and promote *College Dropout* as Rap/Hip-Hop CD of the year. They must have not made it to *Get Em High*, *The New Workout Plan*, or *Breathe In Breathe Out* before making their selection.

That brings us to the question of what is considered Christian and what's not, and is it a necessary category? I know, that was more than one question. Jay Electronica has a song called, *A.P.I.D.T.A.* (All Praise is Due to Allah), but he's not

---

[15] Charles Aaron, "The Spin Interview: 50 Cent (Bigger, Longer, and Uncut)," SPIN (Spin Magazine, May 28, 2019), https://www.spin.com/2007/07/spin-interview-50-cent-bigger-longer-and-uncut/.

considered a five percent rapper. He just raps! And incidentally, many artists pray before a concert and thank God when accepting awards, regardless of their music's content. But they're still just considered artists.

Kendrick Lamar once told the New York Times, when it comes to his fans, "I'm the closest thing to a preacher that they have…My word will never be as strong as God's word. All I am is just a vessel, doing his work."[16]

Lecrae has tried to bend the stereotype of a Christian rapper by proclaiming to be a rapper that happens to be Christian, which is fine in my book, but gets muddy for others. If I'm just one, it may prevent me from being the other. And while many churches rejected Christian rap early on, they're still not too warm on it now. Many believe that while we are supposed to be separate from the world, Christian hip-hop flies too close to the sun.

This may also lend to the fact that when Christian rap events/concerts are held, they're primarily held "outside" of churches. It is interesting to note, two centuries ago, African-Americans were an alien presence in many Christian

---

[16] Joe Coscarelli, "Kendrick Lamar on His New Album and the Weight of Clarity," The New York Times (The New York Times, March 16, 2015), https://www.nytimes.com/2015/03/22/arts/music/kendrick-lamar-on-his-new-album-and-the-weight-of-clarity.html.

congregations, and how, two centuries later, gospel rappers found themselves in the same place.[17]

Why you got a Jesus piece?

In their book, *Perimeters of Light*, authors Ed Stetzer and Elmer Towns created a litmus test to determine if a song was Christian. This was initially meant for progressive churches that were experimenting with their worship sets and drawing concern from older, more traditional church-goers. But let's see how well it stacks up to Christian hip-hop.

First is **The Message Test** – Does this song express the word of God? This test alone would cancel out some gospel songs as well. But that's for another book.

Then **The Purpose Test** – What is the purpose of this music? What emotions do the song want you to convey?

The Association Test – Does the song unnecessarily identify with things, actions or people that are contrary to scripture? An otherwise good song may have to be rejected simply because people will make inappropriate associations with it in their minds. An example of this would be singing/rapping Godly lyrics over a known, "worldly" instrumental.

---

[17] Allen and Strachan, p.7.

The Memory Test – Does the song bring back memories from your past that you have left? This is referred to as a trigger.

The Proper Emotions Test – Does the music stir our negative or lustful feelings? Are we drawn to God or drawn away from Him?

The Understanding Test – Will the listeners have a hard time understanding the message or finding the melody? This will mostly apply to culture and context.

And lastly, **The Music Test** – This test asks if there is really "a song within the song"? Is the song singable? Culturally, African-Americans have been able to take a song that was previously considered dry and leave you in tears (i.e. Marvin Gaye's or Whitney Houston's rendition of the National Anthem).[18]

If you hold up the current market of Christian hip-hop to this test, much of it would not pass. But it is those same failures that is drawing in those that may be tired of the same messages repeated in every mainstream song. When I see collectives like the 116 Clique, it reminds me of the Native Tongues and Dip Set movements. And there are those, like myself, who are used to a certain swag, style and demeanor that hip-hop brings. And

---

[18] Elmer L. Towns and Ed Stetzer, *Perimeters of Light: Biblical Boundaries for the Emerging Church* (Chicago, IL: Moody Publishers, 2004).

that becomes a draw to at least investigate and hear their message. And it doesn't hurt that they can actually rap!

The non-traditional, progressive church in which I pastor is located in a traditional, conservative city. What makes this even more interesting, my congregation is primarily African-American. However, we don't operate like a stereotypical, traditional African-American church. We have been told we draw certain similarities to our white counterparts. That being said, we have discovered we are too black to be a white church and too white to be a black church. When it comes to Christian rap or Holy Hip-Hop, the artist and the genre as a whole are stuck on a similar island battling themselves because they're too holy to be just rap, but not holy enough to be truly Christian.

In speaking of Monica Miller, Erika Gault and Travis Harris provide something else to be considered:

> In Monica Miller's ground-breaking text Religion and Hip Hop, she posits that scholars usually ask the question what is religious about music. It is this formulation that leads to identifying what is considered "sacred" and what is considered "secular." Miller reveals that the art, in and of itself, is not "sacred" or "secular, but rather what the scholar, and in our case, practitioners, fans, and music industry proclaim to be sacred or secular. These shifting and false identifications are primarily made from the perspective of the same White Protestantism that demonized Africans. As a result, "secular" is mostly associated with non-White Protestants. In

the very way that Africanized aesthetics have been characterized as evil or backwards, the African aesthetics in Hip Hop are being identified as "secular."

As a result, a false dichotomy of "sacred" and "secular" rap music is created and produced by "sacred" and "secular" artists that is primarily being judged by a White supremacist criterion.[19]

In his book, *Emotionally Healthy Spirituality*, Peter Scazzero details symptoms of emotionally *unhealthy* spirituality. One of those symptoms is dividing our lives into "secular" and "sacred" compartments. Meaning, I easily compartmentalize God to "Christian activities" while usually forgetting about him when I am working, shopping, studying, or recreating.[20] Ron Sider takes this notion a step further when he states, "Whether the issue is marriage and sexuality or money and care for the poor, evangelicals today are living scandalously unbiblical lives....The data suggest that in many crucial areas evangelicals are not living any differently from their unbelieving neighbors."[21] So when someone says they cannot be a part of my church because I may use "secular" music to illustrate a point,

---

[19] Gault and Harris, p.20.

[20] Peter Scazzero, "The Problem of Emotionally Unhealthy Spirituality," in *Emotionally Healthy Spirituality: It's Impossible to Be Spiritually Mature, While Remaining Emotionally Immature* (Grand Rapids, MI: Zondervan, 2017), p. 30.

[21] Ronald J. Sider, "The Depth of Scandal," in The Scandal of the Evangelical Conscience: Why Are Christians Living Just like the Rest of the World? (Grand Rapids, MI: Baker Books, 2005), pp. 28-29.

my response is, "well, you have on secular clothes, so I guess we're both going to hell."

God did not call the church to be a critic. God called the church to be the example. I have to make sure I'm pushing people closer to God and not further away from Him.

Music producer extraordinaire, Zaytoven, can be credited for creating the current sound of Atlanta. He has curated hits for everyone from the Migos, to Usher, to Mr. Guwop himself, Gucci Mane. But he also has an album with Lecrae and plays keys at his church. How do you classify someone that doesn't cuss, drink or smoke, but happens to make trap music? Particularly when he says things like, "I feel like God put me in this position maybe because of my character, or because I can influence people in a certain way."[22]

Maybe the church is missing the opportunity to provide a powerful statement of faith, placed in a prominent location, to capture the attention of *millions* of Christians.

Unsolicited name drops: Shout out to KB, Bizzle, D-Maub, Dee-1, K-Drama, Blow, Steven Malcolm, Propaganda, Derek

---

[22] Christina Lee, "And on the Seventh Day Zaytoven Became the Lord of Trap Music," Red Bull (The Red Bulletin, August 21, 2018), https://www.redbull.com/us-en/theredbulletin/zaytoven-trap-interview.

Minor, Tedashii, Da' T.R.U.T.H., Trip Lee, Aaron Cole, Wande and Jin

STUNTIN' LIKE MY DADDY

First things first: rest in peace Uncle Phil
For real
You the only father that I ever knew

J. Cole, *No Role Modelz*[1]

Music has the power to communicate, the power to inspire, and the power to change. Music's ability to communicate is so powerful that even the military recognizes its importance. It has been said, at the Pentagon's School of Music, it takes fifteen months of instruction to produce one bandleader. By contrast, the Air Force takes thirteen months to train a jet pilot. Let that sink in.

With the birth of television networks MTV, BET and VH1, the development of the internet, and the progress of streaming services, music of all styles is available at a moment's notice.

---

[1] J. Cole et al., *"No Role Modelz"*, released December 2014, track 9 on *2014 Forest Hills Drive*, Dreamville/Roc Nation/Columbia Records, https://genius.com/J-cole-no-role-modelz-lyrics

However, every generation believes their music is better than the generation prior to them. The common argument generally arises between generations due to their beliefs about the quality of their own particular music. Each generation that comes about fails to understand the mentality of the generation after them.

Generations are typically broken down into categories. The "G.I." Generation, give or take a couple years, extends from 1901–1927. These individuals grew up during the Great Depression and also fought during WWII. The majority of this generation is no longer living.

The "Silent" Generation categorizes those born between 1928-1945. This is the Peace Corp. Generation. These are the ones that witnessed the Atomic Bomb.

A more familiar generation are the "Baby Boomers." This is the category of my parents. This is for those born between 1946-1964 and is readily identified with Dr. Spock, Civil Rights, Woodstock, and Vietnam. This is the generation that sported afros, wore dashikis and played *I'll Take You There* by the Staples Singers on their record players and 8-tracks. During this time there was live percussion, as well as multi-talented musicians.

My generation, "Generation X," pertains to those born from 1965-1981. Many were born during, and some raised, on Sesame Street. This is the MTV generation. The AIDS crisis became real for this group. And crack cocaine was an epidemic.

This generation sported high-top fades, wore Cross Colors and played *Parents Just Don't Understand* by DJ Jazzy Jeff and the Fresh Prince. We believed Hillman College was a real HBCU!

Rap also emerged as a new sound under this generation. The Boomers criticized this new sound of music because they could not readily identify with it, comprehend it, or even catch up with the linguistic speed of it. So, because this new generation did not feel as if they were understood by the previous generation, they were able to reciprocate their feelings through song to let their parents know that they had no indication as to what was really going on in their lives.

Hip-hop's underlining purpose at that time was to unleash these innermost feelings in a positive manner. At the time, it became the voice on poverty, police brutality, gang violence and apartheid amongst other things.

The Baby Boomers, coincidentally, had a similar sound that their parents didn't understand. Their voice rung out vicariously through the James Browns and Marvin Gayes of the world. They were struggling to find their own identity and place in time. This was the era of rebellion and black power, of empowerment and growth. It was a time of civil unrest. Most would even say, without James Brown, Gil Scott-Heron and the Last Poets, there would be no hip-hop.

The sons and daughters of the Baby Boomers and Generation X are the "Millennials." They were typically born between 1982-2000. And because of the emergence of crack throughout the 1980s, some born into this generation would ultimately become labeled, "crack babies." Many were born without their parents and some were even born addicted to the drugs consumed by their parents. And incidentally, this group is three times the size of the generation before them.

The music of this new generation, in comparison to the generations that preceded them, is even more unintelligible and "coded" with a new slang that doesn't allow those that do not share the same mindset to decipher. Yet, just as Curtis Mayfield spoke to the Boomers and N.W.A. spoke to Gen X, this new sound speaks to Millennials.

Because I do not understand what you are listening to, I can no longer speak on your same level. Thus, I do not know how to approach you concerning the things of life, such as drugs, sex and alcohol. This lack of communication amongst generations now produces a generation gap and this gap has been used throughout time to conquer and divide a people.

In the midst of this generational gap an identity crisis has been born. Because the Millennials were born at such a time, they are a generation that no longer knows who their fathers are. Once again, this is the generation born literally "under the influence." They have lost their fathers/parents to death, drugs and/or the penitentiary. Because they no longer know who they are or where they came from, they are forced to take on the identity of those that are speaking their language.

I think I'm Big Meech.

When we look at the traditional family structure and the order in which God fashioned it to be, you have the father, the mother and then the children. If my job is to destroy the family, then naturally I am going to attack the head and allow the body to fall.

Most problems in our adult lives stem from what Gregory Dickow coined, the "father fracture."[2] There is in every one of our lives, some area that is broken or not right because of the way we were raised or were not raised. When there is disrepair in the relationships we have with our fathers, it leaves a fracture in our souls that shape the way we react in life, shapes the way we treat others and shapes the way we see the world. For some, the scars are devastating.

If there was an occurrence of physical or sexual abuse, it is something many never get over and it keeps them from ever being happy, secure and confident as adults. For others, there is just a deficiency in their lives, something lacking or missing and there is no inner peace or wholeness.

This father fracture is where inferiority and insecurity have the fertile soil to grow up in. If a father abused you, you have the tendency to internalize feelings of self-hatred that can lead to depression and in some cases suicide. Why? Because the

---

[2] Gregory Dickow, "Healing the Father Fracture," Charisma Magazine, February 22, 2013, https://charismamag.com/men-life/gregory-dickow-healing-the-father-fracture/.

one man who was supposed to validate you, confirm you and accept you unconditionally, took something from you. The one who was supposed to give you a healthy identity left you scarred and damaged.

Have you ever noticed how many Spanish names end in the suffix "-ez?" You have Rodriguez, Chavez, Velez, etc. In Old Spanish, "-ez" meant the "son of." Therefore, Gonzalo's son was Gonzalez, and Domingo's son was Dominguez, and so forth.

The Polish operate in the same manner with the suffix "-ski," as well as the Irish with the prefix "O-."

For centuries men have been identified by who their fathers are. But when I no longer know who my father is, who can I attach myself to that will call me their son and call me family?

Fast forwarding to the 21st century, many hip-hop artists take on names, aliases and identities not of who their fathers are, but of who they identify with and with whom they are most closely associated with.

I am now naming myself Scarface. I address myself as Gotti. And I take on the identity of Noriega. This is not a personal attack on "Uncle Face," N.O.R.E. (the other Noriega) or Yo Gotti, but if you asked them, they would tell you they felt as if they had a connection with the struggle of the ones whom they assumed their monikers from.

Notwithstanding, it is important to note, these same artists associate themselves with individuals who throughout history have proven to not think well of or even have regard for African-Americans. An artist will take on an Italian identity when Italians historically never had a good relational history with African-Americans.

I have always been a fan of the Godfather trilogy and how the story of an aging patriarch of an organized crime dynasty transfers control of his clandestine empire to his reluctant son. But when you watch *The Sopranos, Goodfellas, Casino, A Bronx Tale*, and any other time Blacks and Italian-Americans interact in media, of those references, most are from a degrading point of view.

The most telling reference occurs in the *Godfather* scene when the heads of the five families have finally called a truce to discuss the introduction of drugs to the criminal underworld. The Godfather, Vito Corleone, is still against the idea. He, along with some of the other gangsters, thinks selling drugs is "a dirty business."

Eventually, however, practical morality concedes to economics and the families decided that selling drugs would be permitted as long as it is kept away from the schools and not sold to children.

Vito's conclusion: *"In my city, we'll keep the traffic in the dark people, the colored. They're animals anyway so let them lose their souls."*[3] The irony in this is that the same gangsters today's youth hold at such a high esteem predicted the destruction of the same inner-city neighborhoods they reside in.

The trend is to take on the identities of crooks, thieves, drug dealers and all-around tough guys, as if to enhance their credibility amongst others who are also suffering from a "fracture" in their homes.

Rick Ross, nee William Leonard Roberts II, took his on-stage persona from "Freeway" Ricky Ross, a California crack cocaine dealer who partnered with the CIA in a drugs-for-cash scheme that funded an insurgency in Nicaragua. 50 Cent, nee Curtis Jackson, named himself after a Brooklyn, NY stick-up artist, Kelvin "50 Cent" Martin, who robbed and murdered local drug dealers.

As I search for my identity through my father, I search for someone that can understand my struggle, my pain, as well as my insecurities. What is actually taking place is a form of modern-day mental slavery.

During slavery, children were separated from their families. As they were separated and sold to a master, they would take on the name of the individual that now owned them. Because I take on the name of this new family, I associate with them even though deep down they really do not care for my

---

[3] *The Godfather*, directed by Francis Ford Coppola (1972; Paramount 2017), 2hrs., 57 mins., DVD.

well-being, which is proven in the fact that I would never enslave somebody I loved.

Because of a lack of proper education in the school system, the subsequent generations are not being taught about their true nature or identity. They are not being taught what happened prior to the middle passage journey that brought their forefathers to this country. They are not being taught that they are from a royal lineage. They are not being taught that it was the strongest of the assemblage that endured the journey across the Atlantic and because of this it is in their blood to withstand any form of pressure, pain and persecution that comes their way. So, because they do not know this, they are quick to associate with those that mean them no good.

While the rest of society seems to condemn crime, hip-hop tends to glorify it on certain levels. Terms like thugs, gangsters and goons, which have negative connotations in mainstream society, are positive terms in the hip-hop world.

Carter G. Woodson, profoundly asserts in *The Miseducation of the Negro,*

> "When you control a man's thinking you do not
> have to worry about his actions. You do not
> have to tell him not to stand here or go yonder.
> He will find his "proper place" and will stay in
> it. You do not need to send him to the back
> door. He will go without being told. In fact, if
> there is no back door, he will cut one for his

special benefit. His education makes it necessary."[4]

Got royalty inside my DNA.

In an article by Dickow on the subject of the "father fracture," he mentions, "The cry of every human heart is for a father, a father who will give us the confidence and affirmation, security and acceptance we long for."[5]

One of the greatest stories of healing the father fracture actually comes from the animated movie, *The Lion King*. This is the story of a royal father, Mufasa, who is killed and leaves behind a devoted family, which includes his would-be heir to the throne, Simba.

Upon his father's death, Simba goes into exile because he does not feel as if he is equipped enough to handle the responsibility of becoming king, especially since he is led to believe the death and absence of his father is his own fault. He does not believe he possesses the look of a king, nor the sound of a king (remember his weak roar?).

One day, Simba was advised to take a look into a pool of water. At first, Simba sees his own reflection. Then he ultimately sees the face of his father. In that moment, he's

---

[4] Carter Godwin Woodson, *The Mis-Education of the Negro* (Asmara, Eritrea: Africa World Press, 1998).

[5] Dickow, http://www.charismamag.com/life/men/16877-gregory-dickow-healing-the-father-fracture.

reminded by the wise mandrill, Rafiki, "You see, he lives in you!"[6]

Simba hears a familiar voice call his name. He looks up. His father's ghostlike image appears among the stars. He is then directed to "Look inside yourself…Remember who you are."[7] It is at that moment Simba recognizes his strength and even gains the "roar" of confidence that always resided on the inside of him.

Remember, while Simba was in exile, the enemy reigned and the land lay dry and barren. In borrowing phrasing from the story of the Prodigal Son, once Simba "came to himself"[8], he was able to restore the land to its original design.

How do we heal the father fracture? First, release yourself from the guilt of your father's absence. For those that grew up without a father, or maybe your father was there physically, but absent emotionally and spiritually, the best thing he taught you was how NOT to be a father. Or for our ladies, what characteristics to look for in a man.

Secondly, the true Father resides within you!

---

[6] *The Lion King*, directed by Roger Allers and Rob Minkoff, (1994; Walt Disney Pictures 2017), 1 hr., 28 mins., DVD.

[7] *The Lion King*

[8] Luke 15:17 (KJV)

"You are gods, And all of you are sons of the Most High." [9]

"Let us make man in our image" [10]

Being in God's image means we share in God's nature. We need to reconnect where Adam disconnected by believing in who God is. God desires a real relationship with each and every one of us. You have to be able to tell yourself, "If don't nobody else want me, God wants me!"

You do not have to allow yourself to become attached to everybody that shows interest in you. We can experience the overwhelming and unconditional love that God has for us. We can know that the love of the Father is the solution to all fear, depression and insecurity in our lives if we will hear His voice saying, "You are my son, my daughter, I love you, I gave my Son for you, I forgive you, I have chosen you to be my beloved, to be joined to my Son for all eternity."

If we can hear His voice and believe His Word, then it will bring healing of our emotions, healing of our fractured hearts and repair the damage done from not having the right relationship with our earthly father that God meant for us to have.

---

[9] Psa. 82:6 (NASB)

[10] Gen. 1:26 (NASB)

141

There's a story of two brothers whose parents were on drugs. One grew up to be a multimillionaire, the other one was strung out on drugs himself.

Someone interviewed both men and asked the one brother, "How did you end up on drugs?" He stated, "Because both of my parents were on drugs."

They asked the other brother, "How did you end up a multimillionaire?" He replied, "Because both of my parents were on drugs."

One used it as an excuse, the other one used it for fuel. Which one are you going to be?

Everything we celebrate had to be broken somewhere along the way. Everything from cars, to benches, to breakfast. Strong nests are built from broken branches.

Unsolicited name drops: Father MC, Trick Daddy, Grand Daddy I.U., Puff Daddy

LADIES FIRST

Girlfriend, let me break it down for you again
You know I only say it 'cause I'm truly genuine
Don't be a hard rock when you really are a gem

Lauryn Hill, *Doo Wop (That Thing)*[1]

Misogyny is defined as a hatred of, aversion to, or prejudice against women.[2] While that may sound harsh when holding up a mirror against religion, Christianity in particular in this instance, and hip-hop, but there tend to be some strong slants in that direction when you explore the historical timeline of both.

When examining the creation narrative, we see over a six-day period where God creates the world as we know it. After every day He creates something, He pauses to evaluate what He created and calls it good. He does this on day one. He does this

---

[1] Lauryn Hill, "*Doo Wop (That Thing)*", released July 1998, track 5 on *The Miseducation of Lauryn Hill*, Ruffhouse Records, Columbia Records, https://genius.com/Lauryn-hill-doo-wop-that-thing-lyrics.

[2] Merriam-Webster dictionaries s.v. "misogyny (n.)," accessed, July 6, 2022, https://www.merriam-webster.com/dictionary/misogyny.

on day two. Again, on day three. Repeat the process on day four. And once again for good measure on day five. On the sixth day He creates His most prized possession in the form of (hu)man.

He creates Adam first. He provides Adam with purpose and an assignment. Adam clocks in every day to tend to the Garden of Eden and name the animals.

When God made Adam, He evaluated His creation and decided for the first time that something was NOT good…alone. God is not suggesting that Adam needed company. He created Eve as a compliment to Adam's calling. Adam would have been unable to accomplish the assignment He was created for independent of some assistance. He needed some help!

God's first word on the subject of men and women is that they were equally created in the image of God.[3] Neither received more of the image of God than the other. So, the Bible begins with the equality of the sexes.

The general position of egalitarianism suggests that there are no biblical, gender-based restrictions between men and women. Their roles can be interchanged. Complementarianism, on the other hand, believes God created two different genders that are equal in value, equally loved by God, but created differently and distinctively to "compliment" one another. And each of them brings something different to the table that cannot be replaced by the other gender. Which is the correct theory is a

---

[3] Gen. 1:27 (NIV)

common debate amongst Christian circles. But just because they were created equal does not mean they are treated equal.

Throughout the Old Testament, women were active in the religious life of Israel. Women played music in the sanctuary[4], prayed there[5], sang and danced with men in religious processions[6], and participated in music and festivities at weddings[7].

However, women typically were not leaders. Women such as Miriam, Deborah and Huldah were more exceptions than the rule.

The New Testament role of women shifts to almost entirely within the scope of the private family. Customarily, a woman of stature could not engage in commerce and would rarely be seen outside her home. If a woman was ever in the streets, she was to be heavily veiled and was prohibited from conversing with men. "As Zhava Glaser gleaned from the Bereshit Rabbah and the Taanit, 'It is the way of a woman to

---

[4] Psa. 68:25 (NIV)

[5] 1 Sam. 1:12 (NIV)

[6] 2 Sam. 6:19, 22 (NIV)

[7] Song of Sol. 2:7; 3:11

stay at home and it is the way of a man to go out into the marketplace'. (Bereshit Rabbah 18:1; cf. Taanit 23b)."[8]

Similarly, Islam asserts the equality of men and women in their creation, but it has been the cross section of history, culture and religion that has brought about oppressive practices and stereotypical views.

The veil worn in Islam is often seen in the West as a symbol of Muslim women's subordinate position in society, but its meaning and use vary enormously in Muslim societies. Historically, the veil has been related to social class, not religion. The veil was first adopted from pre-Islamic Byzantine and Persian customs. In most areas, poor and rural women have covered themselves less than urban and elite women. Veiling rules vary from country to country. In the modern period, strict laws about women's dress are often used to emphasize the religious orientation of a particular government, as in Iran or Saudi Arabia. On the other hand, Turkey does not allow women to wear the veil in public offices or universities because the Turkish state is committed to a more secular identity.[9]

---

[8] Jews for Jesus, "The Role of Women in the Bible," Home - Jews for Jesus, July 30, 2020, https://jewsforjesus.org/publications/inherit/the-role-of-women-in-the-bible.

[9] WGBH Educational Foundation, "Global Connections: Roles of Women," PBS (Public Broadcasting Service, 2002), http://www.pbs.org/wgbh/globalconnections/mideast/questions/women/.

While women are the backbone, and more often than not, the lifeblood of the Christian church, it is a male dominated institution. It is extremely patriarchal. While church attendance tends to heavily favor women, the pastors, priests, deacons, elders and teachers above elementary age are typically men. So, we have made it ok for women to teach our children, but not our adults. More specifically, our men.

Though large numbers of Americans embrace the presence of female leadership at work and in politics, they are least comfortable, comparatively, with women leading the church.[10]

Only female in my crew.

Much like women in the Bible, women in hip-hop don't garner a lot of respect. I know you can point to the MC Lytes, Queen Latifahs, and the Lauryn Hills, yet out of fifty years of production, there is only a handful of female MCs that readily come to people's minds.

Similarly, other than Mary Magdalene, Bathsheba and Rahab (we tend to remember the bad girls), not many women's stories readily come to mind in church either.

As Monica Miller points out, "males created hip-hop and it is still a testosterocentric affair often booming with patriarchal

---

[10] Barna Group, "What Americans Think about Women in Power," Barna Group, March 8, 2017, https://www.barna.com/research/americans-think-women-power/.

ambitions."[11] However, we are living in an age of female empowerment and independence, with a soundtrack being provided by Beyoncé and Meg Thee Stallion. It's less Mary J. Blige and more Latto. For the first time ever, a black female holds the office of Vice President of the United States. Not to be downplayed, black women were credited for carrying the weight of votes to make that happen.

Even though Captain Marvel saved us from Thanos, there is still a steep hill for women to climb. As of 2021, there are 724 billionaires in the United States. On average, that's a new billionaire every seventeen hours. Out of those 724, 86 are women[12], seven of them are black, and only TWO of them are black women (Oprah and Rihanna, last names not even needed).[13] Black lives would not matter so much in the public eye had it not been for black women leading the charge. So, we know women can do anything. That's not up for discussion. It's the notion that that viewpoint is a relatively modern one.

---

[11] Monica R. Miller, Bernard 'Bun B' Freeman, and Anthony B. Pinn, *Religion in Hip Hop* (New York, NY: Bloomsbury Academic, 2015).

[12] Iman Ghosh, "The Richest Women in America in One Graphic," Visual Capitalist, November 23, 2021, https://www.visualcapitalist.com/richest-women-in-america/.

[13] Kerry A. Dolan and Chase Peterson-Withorn, eds., "Forbes Billionaires 2022: The RICHEST PEOPLE IN THE WORLD," Forbes (Forbes Magazine), accessed July 6, 2022, https://www.forbes.com/billionaires/#391dcbae251c.

My earliest recollection of women being on par with men in hip-hop was when MC Lyte released *Eyes on This*. There were substantial accomplishments from other female artists, Lyte included (*10% Dis* and *Paper Thin* are classics!), that occurred prior to this moment in 1989, but for me it was something about that release that made me forget that Lyte was a female. To this day, I can recite *Cha Cha Cha* word-for-word! I substitute "hip male" for "female" and "him" for "her" in the opening bars. And I'm not too shabby on my recitation of *Cappucino* either.

But before MC Lyte became the voiceover for BET award shows, there were women like Roxanne Shanté, Debbie D and Lisa Lee holding their own in the male-dominated sport.

If Kool Herc is credited as one of the originators of hip-hop, the counterpart to his "Adam," naturally has to be an "Eve." Not the pit bull in a skirt from Philly, but rather MC Sha-Rock from the Bronx. Not only was Sha-Rock the first woman to be part of an all-male rap group (The Funky 4 +1), but she also became the first to perform on national television, *Saturday Night Live*, and appear on a cassette tape.

While early hip-hop was about showcasing lyrical ability, post Lyte's first solo project release, there seemed to be a shift that made women the object of an excessive amount of slurs, violence and derogatory statements.

When we run down the list, there's:

"Treat 'em like a prostitute (do what?)/Don't treat no girlie well until you're sure of the scoop" (Slick Rick, *Treat Her Like a Prostitute*)[14]

*"B*****s ain't s*** but hoes and tricks/Lick on these n*** and suck the d***"* (Snoop Dogg, *B*****s Ain't S***)*[15]

"Slut, you think I won't choke no whore/'Til them vocal cords don't work in her throat no more?" (Eminem, *Kill You*)[16]

"Put Molly all in her champagne, she ain't even know it/I took her home and I enjoyed that, she ain't even know it" (Rick Ross, *U.O.E.N.O*)[17]

*"I like having relations/I punch a b**** in the head for playing with my patience/I make a local hoe turn hashin had me*

---

[14] Slick Rick, *"Treat Her Like a Prostitute,"* released November 1988, track 1 on *The Great Adventures of Slick Rick*, Def Jam, Columbia Records, https://genius.com/Slick-rick-treat-her-like-a-prostitute-lyrics.

[15] Dr. Dre, et al. *"Bitches Ain't Shit"*, released December 1992, track 16 on *The Chronic*, Death Row Records, https://genius.com/Dr-dre-bitches-aint-shit-lyrics.

[16] Eminem, Dr. Dre and Mel-Man, *"Kill You,"* released May 2000, track 2 on *The Marshall Mathers LP,* Aftermath/Interscope Records, https://genius.com/Eminem-kill-you-lyrics.

[17] Rocko, Rick Ross and Future, *"U.O.E.N.O,"* released March 2013, track 3 on *Gift of Gab 2*, A1 Recordings, https://genius.com/Rocko-uoeno-lyrics.

at the station/They hating saying that I violated my probation" (Juvenile, *Head in Advance*)[18]

"Snatch that b**** out her car through the window/She screamin', I body slam her on the cement/Until the concrete gave and created a sinkhole/Buried the stink ho in it, then paid to have the street repaved" (Eminem, *Love Game*)[19]

Pretty much the entire *As Nasty as They Wanna Be* album by 2 Live Crew.

And I'll toss in No Limit artist Mercedes' cover to her album, *Rear End*, for good measure. I can vividly picture the cover in my mind, but had to look up the actual name of it.

And that's just a brief list and a lot of asterisks.

Eightball and MJG are one of my favorite rap groups of all time, so it was nothing for me to rap alongside them as a teen in 1993 declaring, "A real nigga believe in beatin' them hoes down/Push her head into the wall 'til you hear that crackin' sound." [20] Before I officially enrolled at The Ohio State

---

[18] Juvenile, *"Head in Advance,"* released December 2003, track 14 on *Juve the Great*, Cash Money Records/UTP/Universal Music Group, https://genius.com/Juvenile-head-in-advance-lyrics.

[19] Eminem, et al., *"Love Game,"* released November 2013, track 14 on *The Marshall Mathers LP 2 (Deluxe)*, Aftermath/Shady/Interscope Records, https://genius.com/Eminem-love-game-lyrics.

[20] Eightball and MJG, *"Pimps,"* released August 1993, track 5 on *Comin' Out Hard*, Suave House, https://genius.com/8ball-and-mjg-pimps-lyrics.

University, I was looking for a scholarship to "Break-a-B****
College."

Academy Award-nominated director Ava DuVernay, in
her critique of the *Straight Outta Compton* film, tweeted both
her concern and struggle with the state of hip-hop:

> I saw the cavalier way that women were treated
> in hip hop spaces early on. Window dressing at
> most. Disposable at worst. Yep, that happened."
> She continued also adding, "To be a woman who
> loves hip hop at times is to be in love with your
> abuser. Because the music was and is that. And
> yet the culture is ours. From depictions of the
> origins of 'Bye Felicia' to watching Cube bring
> his wife Kim to business meetings. That's hip
> hop. A curious thing.[21]

And does it count as misogyny when women dance to
the song, or even create it themselves?

> *"When it come to sex don't test my skills/ Cause my head
> game have you head over heels/ Give a nigga the chills, have
> him pay my bills/ Buy matchin' Lambo's with the same color
> wheels."* (Lil' Kim, *Magic Stick*)[22]

---

[21] Ava DuVernay, Twitter post, August 16, 2015, 12:21 p.m.,
https://twitter.com/ava/status/632950326258085888.

[22] Lil' Kim, and 50 Cent, "*Magic Stick*," released March 2003, track
12 on *La Bella Mafia*, Atlan-tic/Queen Bee/Shady/Aftermath,
https://genius.com/Lil-kim-magic-stick-lyrics.

"Make it cream, make me scream/Out in public, make a scene/I don't cook, I don't clean/But let me tell you how I got this ring." (Cardi B, *WAP*)[23]

Let's not forget Lil' Kim's oft-imitated promotional poster for her debut album, *Hardcore*. Some images will stay with me until Jesus' return.

I do not believe any of the aforementioned individuals hate women, but as Adams and Fuller point out, the idea of misogyny in music also involves the "promotion, glamorization, support, humorization, justification, or normalization of oppressive ideas about women. In misogynistic rap music, there are often degrading statements about women in relation to sex, violent actions, reference of women as to a class lower than men or just as objects for men to use."[24]

De'ja Stokes provided a great example of this when she wrote, "In 1993, Queen Latifah dropped the iconic, feminist song *U.N.I.T.Y* in response to all the male emcees calling

[23] Cardi B, et al., *"WAP,"* released August 2020, Atlantic Records, https://genius.com/Cardi-b-wap-lyrics.

[24] Terri M. Adams and Douglas B. Fuller, "The Words Have Changed but the Ideology Remains the Same: Misogynistic Lyrics in Rap Music," *Journal of Black Studies* 36, no. 6 (July 1, 2006): pp. 938-957, https://doi.org/10.1177/0021934704274072.

females out of their name in their lyrics. But even then, the song did not receive a lot of recognition on the radio."[25]

It is still commonplace for men to refer to women as "the B word" (rhymes with snitch). It is just as commonplace as hearing black men call other black men, "the N word" (rhymes with jigga). We readily hear it in our movies, our TV shows and our music. But misogyny and the like did not start in hip-hop. It is simply perpetuated there.

Thirty-two flavors of that bootylicious bubblegum.

Ronald Weitzer and Charis Kubrin seem to point to a source for this vitriol against women when they state, "artists do not work in a vacuum. We suggest that rappers whose songs portray women negatively are influenced by three major social forces: larger gender relations, the music industry, and local neighborhood conditions."[26]

However, what is not mentioned as a factor is spirituality. The Bible is chauvinistic at its best. It must be understood, the Bible was written for us, not to us. When the Bible was written, the 19th amendment was not thought about. Sojourner Truth had not delivered her speech, "Ain't I a Woman." Nor had Ruth

---

[25] De'ja Stokes, "The Harsh Reality of Misogyny in Hip-Hop," *Journey Magazine*, August 18, 2020, https://jmagonline.com/articles/the-harsh-reality-of-misogyny-in-hip-hop/.

[26] Ronald Weitzer and Charis E. Kubrin, "Misogyny in Rap Music," *Men and Masculinities* 12, no. 1 (2009): pp. 3-29, https://doi.org/10.1177/1097184x08327696.

Bader Ginsburg, colloquially known as the Notorious RBG, been selected to the Supreme Court.

In the time in which the Bible was written, people adhered to a certain set of beliefs. This is not an excuse for calling women out of their names or relegating them to objects of sexual gratification, but merely an opportunity to look at it through a different lens.

Adam and Eve end up getting served an eviction notice from Eden for eating the forbidden fruit, and from that point on men and women have been unable to live and operate peacefully with each other. Can I get an amen from the married section? Before God even doled out His punishments, Adam had already put the blame on "this woman you gave me."[27]

Eve made one colossal mistake that we teach our children when they're very young—don't talk to strangers! It all went left when Eve entertained a conversation she should have shut down. And while we know it was Eve that ate the fruit, let's not forget, Adam ate some as well. In fact, while Eve was entertaining company with a snake, Adam was present. And to equalize the blame a little more, it was to Adam whom God gave the initial instructions, which is why his punishment was probably the biggest.

To the woman, God said, "I will greatly multiply Your pain in childbirth, In pain you will bring forth children; Yet your

---

[27] Gen. 3:12 (NLT)

desire will be for your husband, And he will rule over you."[28] So we see where there would be struggle and difficulty during childbirth, but, I want to highlight the power struggle between God's human species that was pronounced and oftentimes overlooked. John Sailhamer summarizes this struggle nicely when he observes:

> In the second half of Gen 3:16, Eve learns that her "desire" will be for her husband, and he will rule over her. The "desire" here is not sexual because intercourse was indispensable for procreation before the Fall. The context of this verse is one of punishment, so the desire in view is bad.
> What kind of desire, then, is this?
> The reader of Genesis is helped in the next chapter where the words "desire" and "rule" appear again in tandem. God tells Cain that sin's "desire is for you, but you must rule over it" (Gen 4:7). The desire is a ruling one, a dominating one. Most likely, then, in 3:16 the desire of the woman toward her husband is a desire to overcome him. The author intended 3:16 and 4:7 to be read together because the latter clarifies the former.[29]

---

[28] Gen. 3:16 (NASB)

[29] John H. Sailhamer, Tremper Longman, and David E. Garland, "Genesis," in *The Expositor's Bible Commentary* (Grand Rapids, MI: Zondervan, 2017), p. 92.

So, is the treatment of women in hip-hop a reflection of the treatment of women in our society? And is that treatment derived from an ongoing power struggle that has existed as long as time?

Hip-hop is thought to be aggressive and masculine, so it becomes less likely for society to accept female rappers doing the job of a man. Early female pioneers discussed issues similar to men — marginalization, oppression, and urban decay. They also rapped about heterosexual courtship from the perspective of women, domestic violence, and sexism, among other issues. Researchers and scholars found that these female rappers tended to present Black women as independent and autonomous in their songs.[30]

So, when Salt-N-Pepa started releasing songs like, *None of Your Business*, *Let's Talk About Sex* and *Shoop*, they ushered sex and female sovereignty into the spotlight. They brought about bold, in your face speech, bravado, and body confidence.

While Salt-N-Pepa may have openly talked sex, they were not overly sexualized in their appearance. However, they did help open the door for the freedom to do both simultaneously. Because sex sells, the price wagered was accepted and earned female MCs accolades, in spite of their skill level. And this is oftentimes done at the behest of a man.

---

[30] Guevara, 1996; Phillips, Reddick-Morgan, & Stephens, 2005; Rose, 1994

Matthew Oware further pushes us to look at this subject when he states, "Female rappers are obviously masters of their sexuality and control their sexual arenas; however, at what expense to women, particularly Black women, does this form of power cost?"[31]

A worthy reply reveals itself in the empowering words of Audre Lorde who wrote,

> "Survival is not an academic skill. It is learning how to take our differences and make them strengths. For the master's tools will never dismantle the master's house…and this fact is only threatening to those women who still define the master's house as their only source of support."[32]

It is hard for female rappers not to address their gender/sexuality in their music because of the culture and stereotypes within the hip-hop industry. It's sort of like a white rapper to not at some point in time address the fact that they're white. Because they are not the dominant culture, the elephant in the room has to be addressed.

---

[31] Matthew Oware, "A 'Man's Woman'? Contradictory Messages in the Songs of Female Rappers, 1992-2000," *Journal of Black Studies* 39, no. 5 (May 29, 2007): pp. 786-802, https://doi.org/10.1177/0021934707302454.

[32] Audre Lorde, "The Master's Tools Will Never Dismantle the Master's House," in *Sister Outsider: Essays and Speeches* (Trumansburg, NY: Crossing Press, 2007), pp. 110-113.

Unsolicited name drops: Shout out to Rapsody, Bahamadia, Nicki Minaj, Roxanne Shante, Jean Grae, Rah Digga, Missy Elliott, Foxy Brown, Remy Ma, Da Brat, Monie Love, Lady of Rage and Lauryn Hill

VICTORY LAP

The sky is falling, the wind is calling
Stand for something or die in the morning

Kendrick Lamar, *HiiiPoWeR*[1]

Those who have matriculated through Sunday School are able to at least paraphrase the story of the three Hebrew boys who were thrown into the fiery furnace. If you didn't know much else, you knew their names: Shadrach, Meshach and Abednego. For the sake of retention, I like to call the last one, "A bad Negro."

However, those are the names their master gave them. Their real names were Hananiah, Mishael, and Azariah, and they were a part of a Babylonian experiment.

During his reign, King Nebuchadnezzar was one of the most powerful people on the planet. He was the Suge Knight of the ancient world. When he would conquer an area, he was known to employ the services of the best of his captives. His

---

[1] Kendrick Lamar and J. Cole, "*HiiiPoWeR*", released April 2011, track 16 on *Section.80*, Top Dawg Entertainment, https://genius.com/Kendrick-lamar-hiiipower-lyrics.

empire brought together people of all different nations and religions.

Around 586 BC, King Nebuchadnezzar besieges Jerusalem and in doing so requests for some of their men (Daniel of lion's den fame, Hananiah, Mishael, and Azariah) to be added to their court and be fed from the royal table—the best food, the finest wine. Nebuchadnezzar was looking to inculcate them into his culture and train them to be an asset to the king's palace.

An attempt was made to assimilate them into the culture of the court, for they were compelled to learn both the language and the literature of the people among whom they now dwelt.

They were to undergo a rigorous three-year course of training, after which they were to enter the king's service. That educational program probably included a study of agriculture, architecture, astrology, astronomy, law, mathematics, and the Akkadian language.

As described by M.K. Asante Jr., in his book, *It's Bigger Than Hip-Hop*, neocolonialism describes "the economic arrangements by which former colonial powers maintain control over their former colonies and create new dependencies."[2] The revolutionary, Che Guevera, breaks it down further by stating,

---

[2] Molefi K. Asante, *It's Bigger than Hip-Hop: The Rise of the Post-Hip-Hop Generation* (New York, NY: St. Martin's, 2009).

We, politely referred to as 'underdeveloped', in truth are colonial, semi-colonial or dependent countries. We are countries whose economies have been distorted by imperialism, which has abnormally developed those branches of industry or agriculture needed to complement its complex economy. 'Underdevelopment', or distorted development, brings a dangerous specialization in raw materials, inherent in which is the threat of hunger for all our peoples. We, the 'underdeveloped', are also those with the single crop, the single product, the single market. A single product whose uncertain sale depends on a single market imposing and fixing conditions. That is the great formula for imperialist economic domination.[3]

A colony is part of an empire and so colonialism is closely related to imperialism. The colonial powers are typically referred to as Britain, France, Spain and Portugal. But even before them, Daniel dreamed a dream concerning Babylon, Medo-Persia, Greece and Rome.[4]

Consequently, there are three major music labels that control the majority of the music we hear on a regular basis (four until 2012). Those labels, known as the "Big Three," in size

---

[3] Che Guevara, "Cuba: Historical Exception or Vanguard in the Anticolonial Struggle?," Marxists Internet Archive, accessed July 13, 2022, https://www.marxists.org/archive/guevara/1961/04/09.htm.

[4] Dan. 2 (NASB)

order are, Universal Music Group, Sony Music Group and Warner Music Group.

Artists who are signed to one of these major record labels are either signed to the central label or signed to a subsidiary of that label. An artist/group might be signed to Sony, or it might be signed to Columbia Records, which is a Sony subsidiary. These subsidiary labels have their own staff, they sign their own artists, and they make most of their own financial decisions, but in the end, they must answer to their parent company. [5]

Asante further points out, just as the colonial powers were considered the "mother" countries to their particular areas of conquest, the "Big Three" are oftentimes referred to as the "parent" company of their subsidiary labels. So, in spite of the claims that your favorite rapper is a "boss" when it comes to their particular label, they are merely children to a much stronger parent.

The global music business still comprises a powerful oligopoly—a market condition in which a few firms dominate most of an industry's production and distribution. The global reach of these few companies means that they have the

[5] Heather McDonald, "How the Big Four Record Labels Became the Big Three," The Balance Careers (The Balance Careers, July 29, 2019), https://www.thebalancecareers.com/big-three-record-labels-2460743.

promotion and marketing muscle to determine which types of music reach listeners' ears and which become obsolete.[6]

A marionette is a puppet controlled from above using strings. What's funny, but not actually, the individual that controls the puppet is referred to as a "manipulator."

Pieces in one big chess game.

Shortly after appointing "The Hebrew Crew" to positions of power, Nebuchadnezzar made a massive golden statue, and commanded people of all nations to bow down and worship it—or else be thrown into a furnace. Nebuchadnezzar then called his satraps, prefects, governors, counselors, treasurers, judges, and magistrates together. In essence he was calling on all of his officials that had influence over their particular areas to get his message out.

Nebuchadnezzar figured, if he could bring these officials to pay homage to his golden image, the inferior people would of course follow. In obedience to the king's summons, all the magistrates and officers of that vast kingdom left the services of their particular countries, and went to Babylon, to the dedication

---

[6] University of Minnesota, "6.4 Current Popular Trends in the Music Industry," Understanding Media and Culture (University of Minnesota Libraries Publishing edition, 2016. This edition adapted from a work originally produced in 2010 by a publisher who has requested that it not receive attribution., March 22, 2016), https://open.lib.umn.edu/mediaandculture/chapter/6-4-current-popular-trends-in-the-music-industry/.

of this golden image. And it was at the sound of the music that everyone was to bow in reference to this idol.

> A herald then proclaimed in a loud voice: "Attention, everyone! Every race, color, and creed, listen! When you hear the band strike up— all the trumpets and trombones, the tubas and baritones, the drums and cymbals—fall to your knees and worship the gold statue that King Nebuchadnezzar has set up.[7]

The "Big Three," as parents, and just as Nebuchadnezzar, control the message that will be distributed to millions every day. Anyone that defies the rules will be ostracized, dealt with, or in Nebuchadnezzar's terms, placed in the fiery furnace.

The parent company will "raise up" a few (insert any mainstream artist) for the sole purpose of using them to distribute the message they want to be heard by the masses. That is why you do not often hear songs on the radio telling children to go to school, get good grades, or to be respectful. Instead you get a steady stream of misogyny, genocide, drug tales and sexual innuendos. And if ever any mainstream artist decides to do multiple songs to uplift a generation, their level of play on radio stations and streaming channels will substantially decrease.

> "If skills sold, truth be told, I'd probably be
> lyrically Talib Kweli
> Truthfully I wanna rhyme like Common Sense

---

[7] Daniel 3:4,5 (MSG)

But I did 5 mill' – I ain't been rhyming like
Common since."
— Jay Z, Moment of Clarity[8]

Since the early 1930s, five families have run New York's Italian-American Mafia. The five families that I speak of are the Bonanno, the Gambino, the Colombo, the Genovese and the Lucchese families. These particular families were responsible for the establishment of The Commission, a council that would oversee all mafia activities in the U.S. and serve to mediate conflicts between families. At the same time, they would be responsible for all activity that took place by establishing territories. In essence, nothing went down without one of these families being involved. The difference between these families and the ones mentioned earlier is, the Italian bosses controlled most of New York, while the Big Three control the world.

If you look at media as a whole—movies, music, television, radio, internet—there is essentially a Fab Five of sorts that controls everything. Truthfully, it's more like six, but I like my Fab Five reference better.

Ben Bagdikian, points out in his book, *The New Media Monopoly*, "it would have been difficult to imagine in 1983 that the corporations that owned all the country's dominant mass media would, in less than twenty years, shrink from fifty

---

[8] Jay-Z, et al., "*Moment of Clarity*," released November 2003, track 8 on *The Black Album*, Rock-a-Fella Records and Def-Jam Recordings, https://genius.com/Jay-z-moment-of-clarity-lyrics.

separate companies to five."[9] A handful of multinational corporations control nearly everything we see and hear on the screen, over the airwaves and in print, making them a powerful force in shaping contemporary American life.

When it comes to our exposure to the things of this world, it's easy to blame those that are affecting society. If I'm upset about drugs, I blame the local drug dealer. If I'm upset about alcohol, I blame the local liquor store. If I'm upset about today's musical influence, I tend to blame the artist producing the lyrics. But truthfully, none of these things would see the light of day unless a "Commission" allowed it.

We have been taught that the stations and channels are simply giving the people what they want, when in reality we have been taught to, in the words of J.D.B. De Bow, "consume what we do not produce and to produce what we do not consume."[10] We have played into the enemy's hands and have begun to worship and idolize evil as soon as the music is played.

Peninsula maybe.

Now the question is, "How do I avoid being infected when influence is all around me?" For years, the church's answer has been to hide out in the church and you will be safe.

---

[9] Ben H. Bagdikian, *The New Media Monopoly* (Boston, MA: Beacon Press, 2007).

[10] James De Bow, *De Bow's Commercial Review of the South & West*, vol. 7-8 (Arkose Press, 2015).

To quote Richie Rich (not the white, cartoon one), "If you scared, go to church."[11]

In John 17, Jesus is in the midst of His prayer for his followers. In this prayer, Christ prays that they all be protected from evil, but not removed from it. From this, the phrase "be in the world, but not of the world"[12] was developed.

Nowhere in the Bible do we see Jesus distancing himself from those that were considered ungodly or sinners. That was the main group of people He hung around! I can only imagine the places Jesus would hang if He currently walked the earth.

When Jesus got betrayed, the Bible says Judas betrayed Him with a kiss.[13] That was his means of identifying Him. So, if Peter, James, John and Jesus are standing beside each other, you mean to tell me you can't look at them and tell which one is which? Why did Judas have to identify Him with a kiss? Because Jesus looked like everybody else. He didn't have a Jesus outfit.

Jesus was in the people business whose mission, according to Isaiah 61, was to "bring good news to the poor, to

---

[11] 2Pac, Richie Rich and Doug Rasheed, *"Ratha Be Ya Nigga,"* released February 1996, track 23 on *All Eyez On Me*, Deathrow Records and Interscope Records, https://genius.com/2pac-ratha-be-ya-nigga-lyrics.

[12] John 17:14-15 (NASB)

[13] Matt. 26:48 (NASB)

comfort the brokenhearted and to announce that captives will be released and prisoners will be freed."[14]

Immigration has taught us that it is possible to live in a country, learn the language, understand the culture, but never take up residency or declare citizenship. For decades, people from different countries traveled to "the land of the free and home of the brave" simply for opportunity in a free market. They would pick out land, establish a business and then take the profits to support their own particular group of people. Their primary concern was not adapting to their new environment so much so that they would assimilate. Their primary concern was sticking to their original game plan to prosper and build up their family.

Churches can no longer afford to isolate themselves from the communities that they are supposed to be serving. God is in competition with the rest of the world. There are the obvious lures of sex, drugs and alcohol, but despite the known results of fast living, great promotion and advertising makes it all look so good.

The Bible is one of the most entertaining books you can read. It is filled with sex, murder, sex, strippers and oh, did I mention sex? It is our churches that have made it boring. This is where the church has to reevaluate and adjust what it has been doing up to this point, and from there execute a plan of attack.

---

[14] Isa. 61:1 (NLT)

It's the methodology behind our theology. Methodology is our method for getting the theology out. The message doesn't have to change, but the method has to.

The church has lost influence over the years because it has lost its voice in the communities that it is supposed to be comprised of. In many of these communities we see drug dealers, prostitutes, pimps and gangs. On the contrary, God sees people willing to stay out all night doing something they believe in. God sees young men with leadership and administration skills. God sees people that are persuasive in their conversations.

When it came down to God choosing David to be king of Israel, David's family saw him as nothing more than a little brother, a sheep herder, as the youngest and the smallest. His father overlooked him. His brothers overlooked him. Samuel overlooked him. Even Goliath overlooked him. Others saw David as a finished project, but God saw him as being under construction.

How many kings has the church overlooked? What is scary, some of the same people that are wielding influence outside of the church were at one time or another products of the church. Somewhere in the midst of it all we lost our ability to communicate to them because we failed to keep up with the changing language that they were speaking.

God enlisted Moses to communicate a message to Pharaoh as well as to the children of Israel. The problem was, Moses was a poor communicator.

10 But Moses pleaded with the Lord, "O Lord, I'm not very good with words. I never have been, and I'm not now, even though you have spoken to me. I get tongue-tied, and my words get tangled."
11 Then the Lord asked Moses, "Who makes a person's mouth? Who decides whether people speak or do not speak, hear or do not hear, see or do not see? Is it not I, the Lord? 12 Now go! I will be with you as you speak, and I will instruct you in what to say."
13 But Moses again pleaded, "Lord, please! Send anyone else." [15]

Moses has been charged by God to deliver a message to Pharaoh. He is apprehensive about getting the message out. He complains about lack of eloquence. God's answer: I will help you.

The words of Moses to God, if translated literally, would be as follows: "Not a man of words I...for heavy of mouth and heavy of tongue I." Moses's words to God have been translated differently in the various English versions:

"I am not a man of words; I have never been so, and am not now, even after what you have said to your servant: for talking is hard for me, and I am slow of tongue."[16]

---

[15] Ex. 4:10 (NLT)

[16] Ex.4:10 (BBE)

"I'm a terrible speaker. I always have been, and I'm no better now, even after you've spoken to your servant! My words come slowly, my tongue moves slowly."[17]

"I have never been eloquent– either in the past or recently or since You have been speaking to Your servant– because I am slow and hesitant in speech."[18]

"I'm not a good speaker. I've never been a good speaker, and I'm not now, even though you've spoken to me. I speak slowly, and I become tongue-tied easily."[19]

"Lord, I've never been a good speaker. And I haven't gotten any better since you spoke to me. I don't speak very well at all."[20]

"I'm not very good with words. I never have been, and I'm not now, even though you have spoken to me. I get tongue-tied, and my words get tangled."[21]

---

[17] Ex. 4:10 (CJB)

[18] Ex. 4:10 (HCSB)

[19] Ex. 4:10 (GWN)

[20] Ex. 4:10 (NIrV)

[21] Ex. 4:10 (NLT)

These translations have one thing in common: they emphasize that Moses was a poor communicator.[22]

In his commentary on Exodus, when dealing with Moses' speech problem, Adam Clark wrote:

> It is possible he was not intimately acquainted with the Hebrew tongue, so as to speak clearly and distinctly in it. The first forty years of his life he had spent in Egypt, chiefly at court; and though it is very probable there was an affinity between the two languages, yet they certainly were not the same. The last forty he had spent in Midian, and it is not likely that the pure Hebrew tongue prevailed there, though it is probable that a dialect of it was there spoken. On these accounts Moses might find it difficult to express himself with that readiness and persuasive flow of language, which he might deem essentially necessary on such a momentous occasion; as he would frequently be obliged to consult his memory for proper expressions, which would necessarily produce frequent hesitation, and general slowness of utterance, which he might think would ill suit an ambassador of God.[23]

Moses did not suffer from a speech impediment. He more so lacked the ability to communicate properly to a

---

[22] Claude Mariottini, "Did Moses Have a Cleft Lip?," Dr. Claude Mariottini - Professor of Old Testament, May 22, 2014, https://claudemariottini.com/2010/01/18/did-moses-have-a-cleft-lip/.

[23] Adam Clarke and Ralph Earle, *Adam Clarke's Commentary on the Bible* (Grand Rapids, MI: Baker Book House, 1967).

generation of people that spoke differently than he did. Once we lose the ability to communicate, we also lose our ability to influence. And not only that, we lose our ability to go beyond the surface of a generation's issues and tap into their inner emotions. Now is the time that the spiritual community has to place a hedge about our households. Leave your churches and tend to your first church...your home. This would be a good place to quote Big Rube (*True Dat*) when he says, "Take back your existence or die like a punk."[24]

Mamba out. ✌

[24] OutKast, et al., "*True Dat (Interlude),*" released April 1994, track 13 on *Southernplayalisticcadillacmuzik*, LaFace Records and Arista Records, https://genius.com/Outkast-true-dat-interlude-lyrics.

PRODUCTION CREDITS

This book would not have been possible without first, God, whose sense of humor is an acquired taste. Only You would take a kid that didn't like church or school and allow him to pastor one and become a product of higher education.

Secondly, my amazing help meet, Kisha. You constantly remind me of my greatness and potential and that open doors should be expected. You are the true definition of Proverbs 18:22.

To my favorite son, Michael, and my favorite daughter, Madison. You are my broke best friends that never pick up the tab. Thank you for bringing me balance.

To the entire Light of the World Church family. Thank you for following me as I follow Him.

WORKS CITED

Foreword

Scarface, Kelly Price and T-Mix. "What Can I Do". Released August 6, 2002. Track 7 on *The Fix*. The Island Def Jam Music Group. https://genius.com/Scarface-what-can-i-do-lyrics.

Franklin, C.L. *The King Lord of Hosts/ King of the Jews*. 2008. Gospel AIR Records & Tapes AIR7047. Compact disc.

Rock, Pete and C.L. Smooth. "They Reminisce Over You (T.R.O.Y.)". Released April 1994. Track 10 on *Mecca and The Soul Brother*. Elektra Entertainment Group & Elektra Records. https://genius.com/Pete-rock-and-cl-smooth-they-reminisce-over-you-troy-lyrics.

2Pac, Prince Ital Joe and Hurt-M-Badd. "Blasphemy". Released 1996. Track 8 on *The Don Killumanati: The 3 Day Theory*. Death Row Records & Interscope Records. https://genius.com/2pac-blasphemy-lyrics.

Jay-Z, Dan Walsh, Michael Price and Kanye West. "Heart of the City (Ain't No Love)". Released September 11, 2001. Track 8 on *The Blueprint*. Roc-A-Fella Records. https://genius.com/Jay-z-heart-of-the-city-aint-no-love-lyrics.

Prelude

Common and No I.D. "I Used to Love H.E.R.". Released September 1994. Track 2 on *Resurrection*. Relativity Records. https://genius.com/Common-i-used-to-love-her-lyrics.

Minor, Derek. "Fresh Prince." Released June 30, 2017. Derek Minor's House. https://genius.com/Derek-minor-fresh-prince-lyrics.

McIntyre, Hugh. "Report: Hip-Hop/R&B Is the Dominant Genre in the U.S. for the First Time." Forbes. Forbes Magazine, July 17, 2017. https://www.forbes.com/sites/hughmcintyre/2017/07/17/hip-hoprb-has-now-become-the-dominant-genre-in-the-u-s-for-the-first-time/.

Levy, Clifford J. "Harlem Protest of Rap Lyrics Draws Debate and Steamroller." The New York Times, June 6, 1993. https://www.nytimes.com/1993/06/06/nyregion/harlem-protest-of-rap-lyrics-draws-debate-and-steamroller.html.

Genesis

Shan, MC and Marley Marl. "The Bridge". Released August 1987. Track 3 on *Down By Law*. Cold Chillin'/Warner Bros. Records. https://genius.com/Mc-shan-the-bridge-lyrics.

Miller, Monica R., Bernard 'Bun B' Freeman, and Anthony B. Pinn. *Religion in Hip Hop*. New York, NY: Bloomsbury Academic, 2015.

Pinn, Anthony B. *Noise and Spirit: The Religious and Spiritual Sensibilities of Rap Music.* New York, NY: New York University Press, 2003.

Bradley, Adam, and Andrew Lee Dubois, eds. *The Anthology of Rap, 23.* New Haven, CT: YALE University Press, 2011.

Alec. "1970s New York Was an Absolutely Terrifying Place: 41 Photos." All That's Interesting, April 16, 2016. https://allthatsinteresting.com/1970s-new-york-photos.

Genius. "Song Lyrics & Knowledge: Rapper's Delight." Genius. Accessed July 13, 2022. https://genius.com/annotations/20596/standalone_embed?dark=1.

Hirsch, E. D., William G. Rowland, and Michael Stanford. *The New First Dictionary of Cultural Literacy: What Your Child Needs to Know.* Boston, MA: Houghton Mifflin, 2004.

Gault, Erika, and Travis Harris, eds. *Beyond Christian Hip Hop: A Move toward Christians and Hip Hop.* London; New York: Routledge, Taylor et Francis Group, 2021.

Stranded on Death Row

2Pac, Mike Mosley, Big Skye and E.D.I. Mean. "Good Life". Released March 2001. Track 5 on *Until the End of Time.* Amaru Entertainment/Death Row Records and Interscope Records. https://genius.com/2pac-good-life-lyrics.

Lamar, Kendrick, Robin Hannibal, Vindal Friss, Lykke Schmidt and Sounwave. "Bitch Don't Kill My Vibe". Released October 2012, Track 2 on *good kid, m.A.A.d city (Deluxe Version)*. Top Dawg Entertainment/Aftermath Entertainment and Interscope Records. https://genius.com/Kendrick-lamar-bitch-dont-kill-my-vibe-lyrics.

Baumeister, Roy F. *Evil: Inside Human Violence and Cruelty*, 13. New York, NY: W.H. Freeman, 2013.

"About the FCC." Federal Communications Commission. Accessed December 5, 2022. https://www.fcc.gov/about/overview.

MPPDA Digital Archive. *"Magna Charta"*. Resolution. Record #365. Frames 3-2396 to 3-2419 from MPPDA Digital Archive, Flinders University Library Special Collections. https://mppda.flinders.edu.au/records/365 (assessed July 14, 2020).

Lanier, Josh. "'The Brady Bunch': Debunking the Myth Show Was First to Feature Couple Sleeping in the Same Bed." Outsider, February 22, 2021. https://outsider.com/entertainment/brady-bunch-debunking-myth-show-first-feature-couple-sleeping-same-bed/.

Romero, Michaela. "Skyrocketing Homicide Rates in 2022 in New Orleans: Murder Capital of the U.S. Report Says." WGNO, September 20, 2022. https://wgno.com/news/louisiana/orleans-parish/skyrocketing-homicide-rates-in-2022-in-new-orleans-murder-capital-of-the-u-s-report-says/.

Guy, Gene Balk / FYI. "Seattle Ranks as Most Medicated Metro for Mental Health Reasons." The Seattle Times. The Seattle Times Company, January 3, 2022. https://www.seattletimes.com/seattle-news/data/seattle-ranks-as-most-medicated-metro-for-mental-health-reasons/.

DePietro, Andrew. "U.S. Poverty Rate by City in 2021." Forbes. Forbes Magazine, November 9, 2022. https://www.forbes.com/sites/andrewdepietro/2021/11/26/us-poverty-rate-by-city-in-2021/?sh=1a1c69075a54.

Dinnanauth, Robin. *Call to Duty: Advanced Warfare*, 26. Woodhaven, NY: Robin Healing Ministries, 2015.

Metro Boomin, Future and Drake. "Jumpman". Released September 2015. Track 9 on *What a Time to Be Alive*. OVO Sound/Republic Records/Young Money/Freebandz/Epic Records and Cash Money Records. https://genius.com/Drake-and-future-jumpman-lyrics.

Centeno, Tony M. "Future Beats Drake's Record to Become Most Platinum Rapper of 2010s." iHeart. iHeartRadio, July 28, 2022. https://www.iheart.com/content/2022-07-28-future-beats-drakes-record-to-become-most-platinum-rapper-of-2010s/.

Johnson, Robert. "Cross Road Blues (Take 1)". Released May 1937. Track 17 on *The Complete Recordings*. Vocalion Records. https://genius.com/Robert-johnson-cross-road-blues-take-1-lyrics.

D.O.C., The, Kurupt and Daz Dillinger. "Murder Was the Case (Death After Visualizing Eternity)". Released November

1993. Track 8 on *Doggystyle*. Death Row Records/Interscope Records and Atlantic Records. https://genius.com/Snoop-dogg-murder-was-the-case-death-after-visualizing-eternity-lyrics.

D'evils

Deep, Mobb. "Survival of the Fittest". Released April 1995. Track 3 on *The Infamous*. BMG Music. https://genius.com/Mobb-deep-survival-of-the-fittest-lyrics.

Heskes, Irene. *Passport to Jewish Music: Its History, Traditions and Culture*, 41. Milwaukee, WI: Hal Leonard, 2002.

Singer, Bryan, director. *The Usual Suspects*. 1995; Gramercy Pictures 2002. 1hr., 46 mins. DVD.

Lopes, Lisa "Left Eye", Rico Wade, Sleepy Brown, Ray Murray and Marqueze Ethridge. "Waterfalls". Released November 1994. Track 8 on *CrazySexyCool*. LaFace Records and Arista Records. https://genius.com/Tlc-waterfalls-lyrics.

National Space and Air Museum. "Waves in the Air." How Things Fly. Accessed July 24, 2022. https://howthingsfly.si.edu/aerodynamics/waves-air.

Weinberger, Ed, Michael Leeson, and Bill Cosby. "The Cosby Show." Episode. A Shirt Story Season 1, Episode 5. New York, NY: NBC, October 18, 1984.

Perez-y-Soto, Danny Grajales. "Counterfeiting and Piracy in 2021 – the Global Impact." Anti-counterfeiting and

Online Brand Enforcement: Global Guide 2021 - World
Trademark Review, May 11, 2021.
https://www.worldtrademarkreview.com/global-
guide/anti-counterfeiting-and-online-brand-
enforcement/2021/article/counterfeiting-and-piracy-in-
2021-the-global-impact.

Tzu, Sun. *The Art of War*. Edited by John Minford. New York,
NY: Penguin Books, 2002.

Daniels, Dharius. *Represent Jesus: Rethink Your Version of
Christianity and Become More like Christ*, 53. Lake
Mary, FL: Passio, 2014.

CNBC.com. "Things Are Looking up in America's Porn
Industry." NBCNews.com. NBCUniversal News Group,
January 20, 2015.
https://www.nbcnews.com/business/business-
news/things-are-looking-americas-porn-industry-
n289431.

Tate, Nick. "Porn Use Spiked during the Pandemic." WebMD,
May 26, 2021.
https://www.webmd.com/lung/news/20210526/porn-use-
spiked-during-the-pandemic.

Follow the Leader

Mike, Killer. "Reagan". Released May 2012. Track 6 on *R.A.P.
Music*. Williams Street. https://genius.com/Killer-mike-
reagan-lyrics.

Stoute, Steve and Mim Eichler Rivas. *The Tanning of America:
How Hip-Hop Created a Culture That Rewrote the Rules*

of the New Economy. New York, NY: Gotham Books, 2012.

Tony Rock, Charlie Mack, & D-Dot | Drink Champs (Full Episode). *YouTube*. Revolt TV, 2018. https://www.youtube.com/watch?v=tiDvgH8yNhg.

Taylor, Carl S., and Virgil Taylor. "Rap Music Provides a Realistic View of Life." Essay. *In Popular Culture: Opposing Viewpoints*, edited by John Woodward. Detroit, MI: Thomson/Gale, 2005.

Diamond, Sarah, Rey Bermudez, and Jean Schensul. "What's The Rap about Ecstasy?" *Journal of Adolescent Research* 21, no. 3 (2006): 269–98. https://doi.org/10.1177/0743558406287398.

Del Barco, Mandalit. "Breakdancing, Present at the Creation." NPR, October 14, 2002. https://news.npr.org/programs/morning/features/patc/breakdancing/index.html.

Cobb, Jelani. *To the Break of Dawn: A Freestyle on the Hip Hop Aesthetic*. New York, NY: New York University Press, 2008.

Caz, Grandmaster, Master Gee, Wonder Mike, Big Bank Hank, Nile Rodgers, Bernard Edwards and Sylvia Robinson. "Rapper's Delight". Released September 1979. Track 6 on Sugarhill Gang. Rhino Entertainment Company/Sugarhill Records Inc./Sugarhill Records. https://genius.com/Sugarhill-gang-rappers-delight-lyrics.

Base, Rob. "It Takes Two". Released August 1988. Track 1 on *It Takes Two*, Profile Records. https://genius.com/Rob-base-and-dj-e-z-rock-it-takes-two-lyrics.

Juvenile, Mannie Fresh and Lil' Wayne "Back That Azz Up". Released November 1998. Track 13 on *400 Degreez*. Universal Recordings and Cash Money Records. https://genius.com/Juvenile-back-that-azz-up-lyrics.

Pat, Project, DJ Paul, La Chat and Juicy J. "Chickenhead". Released January 2001. Track 1 on *Mista Don't Play: Everythangs Working*. Epic/SRC/Hypnotize Minds/Loud Records/RED Distribution. https://genius.com/Project-pat-chickenhead-lyrics.

Flav, Flavor, Gary G-Wiz, Chuck D, Hank Shocklee, Eric Sadler and Keith Shocklee. "Fight the Power". Released June 1989. Track 20 on *Fear of a Black Planet*. Def Jam Recordings. https://genius.com/Public-enemy-fight-the-power-lyrics.

Mix-a-Lot, Sir and Amylia Dorsey-Rivas. "Baby Got Back". Released February 1992. Track 3 on *Mack Daddy*. Def American/Reprise. https://genius.com/Sir-mix-a-lot-baby-got-back-lyrics.

Famuyiwa, Rick, director. *Brown Sugar* 2002; Fox Searchlight Pictures 2003. 1hr., 49 mins. DVD.

George, Nelson. *Buppies, B-Boys, BAPS, and Bohos: Notes on Post-Soul Black Culture*. Cambridge, MA: Da Capo Press, 2001.

Beggs, Scott. "10 Fab Facts about 'Yo! MTV Raps'." Mental Floss, May 2, 2022.

https://www.mentalfloss.com/article/553165/facts-about-yo-mtv-raps.

Jay-Z, Kyambo "Hip Hop" Joshua, Rockwilder, Beanie Sigel and Amil. "Do It Again (Put Ya Hands Up)". Released December 1999. Track 3 on *Vol. 3...Life and Times of S. Carter*. Def Jam Recordings and Roc-A-Fella Records. https://genius.com/Jay-z-do-it-again-put-ya-hands-up-lyrics.

Merriam-Webster dictionaries s.v. "influence (n.)". Accessed, July 25, 2022. https://www.merriam-webster.com/dictionary/influence.

Nas and DJ Premier. "N.Y. State of Mind". Released April 1994. Track 2 on *Illmatic*. Sony Music Entertainment. https://genius.com/Nas-ny-state-of-mind-lyrics.

Nas, AZ, L.E.S., Ronnie Wilson, Olu Dara and Oliver Scott. "Life's a Bitch". Released April 1994. Track 3 on *Illmatic*. Sony Music Entertainment. https://genius.com/Nas-lifes-a-bitch-lyrics.

Muhammad, Ali Shaheed, Q-Tip and Phife Dawg. "Electric Relaxation". Released November 1993. Track 8 on *Midnight Marauders*. Zomba Recording Corporation. https://genius.com/A-tribe-called-quest-electric-relaxation-lyrics.

White, Nicholas. "Music Does More than Hype Athletes, It Helps Prep the Brain for Action." Global Sport Matters, November 25, 2019. https://globalsportmatters.com/health/2019/11/25/music-does-more-than-hype-athletes-it-helps-prep-the-brain-for-action/.

Hybels, Bill, and Mark Mittelberg. *Becoming a Contagious Christian*. Grand Rapids, MI: Zondervan, 2007.

New God Flow. 1

Killah, Ghostface and Mathematics. "Mighty Healthy". Released February 2000. Track 9 on *Supreme Clientele*. Epic/Sony/Razor Sharp, https://genius.com/Ghostface-killah-mighty-healthy-lyrics.

Hackett, Conrad, and David McClendon. "Christians Remain World's Largest Religious Group, but They Are Declining in Europe." Pew Research Center. Pew Research Center, May 31, 2020. https://www.pewresearch.org/fact-tank/2017/04/05/christians-remain-worlds-largest-religious-group-but-they-are-declining-in-europe/.

Miller, Monica R., Anthony B. Pinn, and H. Samy Alim. "Re-Inventing Islam with Unique Modern Tones: Muslim Hip Hop Artists as Verbal Mujahidin." Chapter. In *The Hip Hop and Religion Reader*, 187. New York, NY: Routledge, 2015.

Nicholson, Reynold A. *Literary History of the Arabs*, 62. London: Routledge, 2013.

Muhammad, Ashahed M. "God's Influence In HipHop." The Final Call, July 22, 2014. http://www.finalcall.com/artman/publish/National_News_2/article_101629.shtml.

Miyakawa, Felicia M. *Five Percenter Rap: God Hop's Music*, Message, and Black Muslim Mission. Bloomington, IN: Indiana University Press, 2005.

Quan, Jay. "The 5 Percent Nation's Impact on Hip-Hop's Golden Era." Rock the Bells, 2022. https://rockthebells.com/articles/a-history-of-the-5-percent-nation-the-golden-era-of-hip-hop/.

ionehiphopwiredstaff. "The Gods of Hip-Hop: A Reflection on the Five Percenter Influence on Rap Music & Culture." Hip Hop Wired, March 24, 2010. https://hiphopwired.com/32991/the-gods-of-hip-hop-a-reflection-on-the-five-percenter-influence-on-rap-music-culture/.

Baker, Christian. "Enter the Five Percent: How Wu-Tang Clan's Debut Album Maps the Complex Doctrine of the Five Percent Nation." Center for the Humanities. Washington University in St. Louis Arts and Sciences, May 13, 2020. https://humanities.wustl.edu/news/enter-five-percent-how-wu-tang-clan%E2%80%99s-debut-album-maps-complex-doctrine-five-percent-nation.

Knight, Michael Muhammad. *The Five Percenters: Islam, Hip Hop and the Gods of New York*, 182. Oxford: Oneworld, 2009.

Stetsasonic. "Free South Africa (The Remix)". Released February 1991. Track 17 on *Blood Sweat & No Tears*. Tommy Boy/Warner Bros. Records. https://genius.com/Stetsasonic-free-south-africa-the-remix-lyrics.

Pinn, Anthony B. *Noise and Spirit: The Religious and Spiritual Sensibilities of Rap Music*. New York, NY: New York University Press, 2003.

Adams, Dart. "How Stop the Violence Movement's 'Self Destruction' Became One of the Most Important Rap Releases." Okayplayer, August 11, 2020. https://www.okayplayer.com/music/the-making-krs-one-stop-the-violence-movements-self-destruction-single-89.html.

Muhammad, Cinque. "What Happened to Hip Hop's Social Consciousness?" Austin Weekly News, February 10, 2021. https://www.austinweeklynews.com/2008/07/09/what-happened-to-hip-hops-social-consciousness/.

Ima Boss

Daddy, Puff, The LOX, Notorious B.I.G. and Lil' Kim. "It's All About the Benjamins Remix". Recorded, July 1996. Track 10 on *No Way Out*. Bad Boy Entertainment and Arista Records. https://genius.com/Diddy-its-all-about-the-benjamins-remix-lyrics.

Zollman, Joellyn. "Jewish Immigration to America: Three Waves." My Jewish Learning, May 19, 2017. https://www.myjewishlearning.com/article/jewish-immigration-to-america-three-waves/.

Berlin, Irving, Hannah Arendt, Albert Einstein, Emma Lazarus, Albert Potter, Solomon Smulewitz, Leo Rosenberg, et al. "From Haven to Home: 350 Years of Jewish Life in America a Century of Immigration, 1820-1924." Library of Congress, September 9, 2004. https://www.loc.gov/exhibits/haventohome/haven-century.html.

Kobrin, Rebecca. *Chosen Capital: The Jewish Encounter with American Capitalism*. New Brunswick (NJ): Rutgers University Press, 2012.

Katorza, Ari. *Stairway to Paradise Jews, Blacks, and the American Music Revolution*. Berlin: De Gruyter Oldenbourg, 2021.

"Black Sabbath: The Secret Musical History of Black–Jewish Relations." The CJM, August 26, 2010. https://www.thecjm.org/exhibitions/22.

Killmeier, Matthew A. "Race Music." Encyclopedia.com. St. James Encyclopedia of Popular Culture, June 21, 2022. https://www.encyclopedia.com/media/encyclopedias-almanacs-transcripts-and-maps/race-music.

Dawg, Phife, Ali Saheed Muhammad and Q-Tip. "Check the Rhime". Released September 1991. Track 9 on *The Low End Theory*. Zomba Recording Corporation. Jive Records and RCA Records. https://genius.com/A-tribe-called-quest-check-the-rhime-lyrics.

Ball, Jared. "Hip-Hop's Still Troubled Narrative: A Requiem for C. Delores Tucker." iMWiL!, June 8, 2022. https://imixwhatilike.org/2017/10/28/hip-hops-still-troubled-narrative-requiem-c-delores-tucker-jared-ball/.

"C. Delores Tucker." Biography. Your Dictionary. Accessed July 4, 2022. https://biography.yourdictionary.com/c-delores-tucker.

Ladies First

Hill, Lauryn. "Doo Wop (That Thing)". Released July 1998. Track 5 on *The Miseducation of Lauryn Hill*. Ruffhouse Records. Columbia Records. https://genius.com/Lauryn-hill-doo-wop-that-thing-lyrics.

Merriam-Webster dictionaries s.v. "misogyny (n.)". Accessed, July 6, 2022. https://www.merriam-webster.com/dictionary/misogyny.

Jews for Jesus. "The Role of Women in the Bible." Home - Jews for Jesus, July 30, 2020. https://jewsforjesus.org/publications/inherit/the-role-of-women-in-the-bible.

WGBH Educational Foundation. "Global Connections: Roles of Women." PBS. Public Broadcasting Service, 2002. http://www.pbs.org/wgbh/globalconnections/mideast/questions/women/.

Barna Group. "What Americans Think about Women in Power." Barna Group, March 8, 2017. https://www.barna.com/research/americans-think-women-power/.

Miller, Monica R., Bernard 'Bun B' Freeman, and Anthony B. Pinn. *Religion in Hip Hop*. New York, NY: Bloomsbury Academic, 2015.

Ghosh, Iman. "The Richest Women in America in One Graphic." Visual Capitalist, November 23, 2021. https://www.visualcapitalist.com/richest-women-in-america/.

Dolan, Kerry A., and Chase Peterson-Withorn, eds. "Forbes Billionaires 2022: The RICHEST PEOPLE IN THE

WORLD." Forbes. Forbes Magazine. Accessed July 6,
2022.
https://www.forbes.com/billionaires/#391dcbae251c.

Rick, Slick. "Treat Her Like a Prostitute." Released November
1988. Track 1 on *The Great Adventures of Slick Rick*.
Def Jam, Columbia Records. https://genius.com/Slick-
rick-treat-her-like-a-prostitute-lyrics.

Dre, Dr., Tha Dogg Pound, Jewell and Snoop Dogg. "Bitches
Ain't Shit." Released December 1992. Track 16 on *The
Chronic*. Death Row Records. https://genius.com/Dr-dre-
bitches-aint-shit-lyrics.

Eminem, Dr. Dre and Mel-Man, "Kill You," released May
2000, track 2 on *The Marshall Mathers LP*,
Aftermath/Interscope Records,
https://genius.com/Eminem-kill-you-lyrics.

Rocko, Rick Ross and Future. "U.O.E.N.O." Released March
2013. Track 3 on *Gift of Gab 2*. A1 Recordings.
https://genius.com/Rocko-uoeno-lyrics.

Juvenile. "Head in Advance." Released December 2003. Track
14 on *Juve the Great*, Cash Money
Records/UTP/Universal Music Group,
https://genius.com/Juvenile-head-in-advance-lyrics.

Eminem, Kendrick Lamar, Coy Poe, Jimmie Grier, Pinky
Tomlin and Clint Ballard. "Love Game." Released
November 2013. Track 14 on *The Marshall Mathers LP
2 (Deluxe)*. Aftermath/Shady/Interscope Records.
https://genius.com/Eminem-love-game-lyrics.

Eightball and MJG. "Pimps." Released August 1993. Track 5 on *Comin' Out Hard*. Suave House. https://genius.com/8ball-and-mjg-pimps-lyrics.

DuVernay, Ava. Twitter post. August 16, 2015. 12:21 p.m. https://twitter.com/ava/status/632950326258085888.

_____. Twitter post. August 16, 2015. 12:33 p.m. https://twitter.com/ava/status/632953219824553984?lang =da.

_____. Twitter post. August 16, 2015. 12:35 p.m. https://twitter.com/ava/status/632953804233699328.

Kim, Lil' and 50 Cent. "Magic Stick," released March 2003, track 12 on *La Bella Mafia*, Atlantic/Queen Bee/Shady/Aftermath, https://genius.com/Lil-kim-magic-stick-lyrics.

B, Cardi, Megan Thee Stallion, Frank Rodriquez, Ayo The Producer, Pardison Fontaine and KEYZBABY. "WAP," released August 2020, Atlantic Records, https://genius.com/Cardi-b-wap-lyrics.

Adams, Terri M., and Douglas B. Fuller. "The Words Have Changed but the Ideology Remains the Same: Misogynistic Lyrics in Rap Music." *Journal of Black Studies* 36, no. 6 (July 1, 2006): 938–57. https://doi.org/10.1177/0021934704274072.

Stokes, De'ja. "The Harsh Reality of Misogyny in Hip-Hop." Journey Magazine, August 18, 2020. https://jmagonline.com/articles/the-harsh-reality-of-misogyny-in-hip-hop/.

Weitzer, Ronald, and Charis E. Kubrin. "Misogyny in Rap Music." *Men and Masculinities* 12, no. 1 (2009): 3–29. https://doi.org/10.1177/1097184x08327696.

Sailhamer, John H., Tremper Longman, and David E. Garland. "Genesis." Essay. In *The Expositor's Bible Commentary*, 92. Grand Rapids, MI: Zondervan, 2017.

Oware, Matthew. "A 'Man's Woman'? Contradictory Messages in the Songs of Female Rappers, 1992-2000." *Journal of Black Studies* 39, no. 5 (May 29, 2007): 786–802. https://doi.org/10.1177/0021934707302454.

Lorde, Audre. "The Master's Tools Will Never Dismantle the Master's House." Essay. In *Sister Outsider: Essays and Speeches*, 110–13. Trumansburg, NY: Crossing Press, 2007.

Lord Knows

DMX and Scott Storch. "Lord Give Me a Sign." Released August 2006. Track 15 on *Year of the Dog...Again*. Sony BMG. https://genius.com/Dmx-lord-give-me-a-sign-lyrics.

Oberman, Heiko A. *Luther: Man Between God and the Devil*. New York, NY: Image Books, 1989.

Kramer, Walter, and Gotz Trenkler. "Luther." *Lexicon van Hardnekkige Misverstanden* (Netherlands: Bert Bakker, 1997): 214–16.

Buursma, Bruce. "Parish Running Religion up Ad Flagpole." Chicago Tribune, August 9, 2021.

https://www.chicagotribune.com/news/ct-xpm-1986-10-31-8603220090-story.html.

Wise, Justin. *The Social Church a Theology of Digital Communication*. Chicago, IL: Moody Publishers, 2014.

Pew Research Center. "Christian Traditions." Pew Research Center's Religion & Public Life Project, April 26, 2022. http://www.pewforum.org/2011/12/19/global-christianity-traditions/#protestant.

Allen, Curtis, and Owen Strachan. Foreword. In *Does God Listen to Rap?: Christians and the World's Most Controversial Music*, 7. Adelphi, MD: Cruciform Press, 2013.

Gault, Erika, and Travis Harris. *Beyond Christian Hip Hop: A Move toward Christians and Hip Hop*. New York, NY: Routledge, Taylor et Francis Group, 2021.

Aaron, Charles. "The Spin Interview: 50 Cent (Bigger, Longer, and Uncut)." SPIN. Spin Magazine, May 28, 2019. https://www.spin.com/2007/07/spin-interview-50-cent-bigger-longer-and-uncut/.

Coscarelli, Joe. "Kendrick Lamar on His New Album and the Weight of Clarity." The New York Times. The New York Times, March 16, 2015. https://www.nytimes.com/2015/03/22/arts/music/kendrick-lamar-on-his-new-album-and-the-weight-of-clarity.html.

Towns, Elmer L., and Ed Stetzer. *Perimeters of Light: Biblical Boundaries for the Emerging Church*. Chicago, IL: Moody Publishers, 2004.

Scazzero, Peter. "The Problem of Emotionally Unhealthy Spirituality." Chapter. In *Emotionally Healthy Spirituality: It's Impossible to Be Spiritually Mature, While Remaining Emotionally Immature*, 30. Grand Rapids, MI: Zondervan, 2017.

Sider, Ronald J. "The Depth of Scandal." Chapter. In *The Scandal of the Evangelical Conscience: Why Are Christians Living Just like the Rest of the World?* 28–29. Grand Rapids, MI: Baker Books, 2005.

Lee, Christina. "And on the Seventh Day Zaytoven Became the Lord of Trap Music." Red Bull. The Red Bulletin, August 21, 2018. https://www.redbull.com/us-en/theredbulletin/zaytoven-trap-interview.

Stuntin' Like My Daddy

Cole, J., Phonix Beats, Suga-T, D-Shot, Studio Ton, DJ Paul, Juicy J, E-40 and B-Legit. "No Role Modelz". Released December 2014. Track 9 on *2014 Forest Hills Drive*. Dreamville/Roc Nation/Columbia Records. https://genius.com/J-cole-no-role-modelz-lyrics.

Dickow, Gregory. "Healing the Father Fracture." Charisma Magazine, February 22, 2013. https://charismamag.com/men-life/gregory-dickow-healing-the-father-fracture/.

Coppola, Francis Ford, director. *The Godfather*. 1972; Paramount 2017. 2hrs., 57 mins. DVD.

Woodson, Carter Godwin. *The Mis-Education of the Negro*. Asmara, Eritrea: Africa World Press, 1998.

Allers, Roger and Rob Minkoff, directors. *The Lion King*. 1994; Walt Disney Pictures 2017. 1 hr., 28 mins. DVD

Victory Lap

Lamar, Kendrick and J. Cole. "HiiiPoWeR". Released April 2011. Track 16 on *Section.80*. Top Dawg Entertainment. https://genius.com/Kendrick-lamar-hiiipower-lyrics.

Guevara, Che. "Cuba: Historical Exception or Vanguard in the Anticolonial Struggle?" Marxists Internet Archive. Accessed July 13, 2022. https://www.marxists.org/archive/guevara/1961/04/09.htm.

Asante, Molefi K. *It's Bigger than Hip-Hop: The Rise of the Post-Hip-Hop Generation*. New York, NY: St. Martin's, 2009.

McDonald, Heather. "How the Big Four Record Labels Became the Big Three." The Balance Careers. The Balance Careers, July 29, 2019. https://www.thebalancecareers.com/big-three-record-labels-2460743.

University of Minnesota. "6.4 Current Popular Trends in the Music Industry." Understanding Media and Culture. University of Minnesota Libraries Publishing edition, 2016. This edition adapted from a work originally produced in 2010 by a publisher who has requested that it not receive attribution. March 22, 2016. https://open.lib.umn.edu/mediaandculture/chapter/6-4-current-popular-trends-in-the-music-industry/.

Jay-Z, Luis Resto, Steve King and Eminem. "Moment of Clarity." Released November 2003. Track 8 on *The Black Album*. Rock-a-Fella Records and Def-Jam Recordings. https://genius.com/Jay-z-moment-of-clarity-lyrics.

Bagdikian, Ben H. *The New Media Monopoly*. Boston, MA: Beacon Press, 2007.

De Bow, James. *De Bow's Commercial Review of the South & West*. 7-8. Vol. 7-8. Arkose Press, 2015.

2Pac, Richie Rich and Doug Rasheed. "Ratha Be Ya Nigga." Released February 1996. Track 23 on *All Eyez On Me*. Deathrow Records and Interscope Records. https://genius.com/2pac-ratha-be-ya-nigga-lyrics.

Mariottini, Claude. "Did Moses Have a Cleft Lip?" Dr. Claude Mariottini - Professor of Old Testament, May 22, 2014. https://claudemariottini.com/2010/01/18/did-moses-have-a-cleft-lip/.

Clarke, Adam, and Ralph Earle. *Adam Clarke's Commentary on the Bible*. Grand Rapids, MI: Baker Book House, 1967.

3000, André, Big Boi, Big Rube and Organized Noize. "True Dat (Interlude)." Released April 1994. Track 13 on *Southernplayalisticcadillacmuzik*. LaFace Records and Arista Records. https://genius.com/Outkast-true-dat-interlude-lyrics.

Made in the USA
Middletown, DE
16 August 2024